Günter von Hummel

**The vertikal Ego**

A path to self-analytical practice

The cover picture of the painter T. Heydecker has the title 'Who is speaking me? Who makes that head, implied eyes and all the objects and reflections have a common name, which is me, my Ego? Although much is set up horizontally, in which the pieces of furniture have validity, the picture has a vertical direction, whose I or Ego penetrates everything.

2020 von Hummel, Günter

Production and Publishing: BoD – Books on Demand

ISBN 9783750415492

# Table of Contents

# 1. Reinventing Psychoanalysis

For a long time I have believed that psychoanalysis is a third science that has established itself alongside the natural and human sciences. It is based on the assumption that the nature of man is his relationship to man, and I particularly liked the word nature in it. But then, what is the nature of nature, I thought to myself stupidly and began to question the nature of sciences more closely. It is in line with this that the French psychoanalyst J. Lacan in his twenty-fourth seminar asked himself the question, whether classical psychoanalysis is not based on the nature of an " autism in twos".  Finally, in the psychoanalytic session, the analyst and his patient decide that, although neither of them knows anything about the other and they have no fixed subject matter, they will sit together for a few hundred hours (apparently just each for himself).

So when conventional psychoanalysis behaves like an "autism in twos", it is much like someone who likes to read books goes to a clothing store and asks the salesman for a good novel. These two also face each other with consternation, at first. But perhaps the salesperson mischievously asks back: produced in a soft and warm tone like flannel or cool and light like linen? After all, the two won't be talking so completely at cross purposes. The seller takes the word 'good novel' allegorically, the buyer probably wants a piece of clothing that fits like a 'good novel'. It's about two qualities, good and novelistic, which can be taken like flannel or linen, and on which two strangers, two foreigners, could agree, although they apparently don't speak the same language or - to take up the concept of nature once again - are of different natures.

Quite the opposite is what the science journalist M. Gladwell writes in his latest book, namely that people believe too much of what others, especially strangers, are telling them.[1] They do not come to an agreement with this, but constantly talk past each other, even though they use the same language. They speak, but they say nothing to each other, while the clothes salesman and his customer say much more to each other than is necessary and only need two words (qualities). They seem to have fallen out of time, while the people in Gladwell's bestseller are constantly looking to be at the same level of communicative interaction while applying interrogation, important conversation and abuse assessments.

Before I come back to Gladwell, let's get back to psychoanalysis. In it, two protagonists circle around each other as two unknowns, as in an inaccessible jungle or some other, otherwise completely deserted country, as two autistic people. The survival artist Rüdiger Nehberg once met someone like him in the Brazilian rainforest, but Nehberg didn't have much in his hands, while the other seemed well equipped. Nehberg was at survival training, where you weren't even allowed to carry a knife, so he was a bit in panic. The two greeted each other friendly, but couldn't the other think that Nehberg

---

[1] Gladwell, M., Talking to Strangers (2019)

was carrying enough money with him or that for some other reason nothing could kill him?

No one would know about it, for tens of miles there was no human being. Nehberg resorted to a ruse and called Roberto or Mattheo in a loud voice, as if he were with a friend who was within calling distance. Indicating that he was not alone, he could now exchange a few words with the stranger and get an idea of him, even engage him in a conversation from which he could better assess the person opposite. Even before Roberto or Mattheo had to be called again, they could separate again and wish the stranger good further wanderings. Such behaviour had been exactly the opposite of Gladwell's: Past each other, but for once it went well.

For Gladwell is of the opinion that most people are in a precarious "truth mode" in which, as I said, you first believe everything that the other person, especially the stranger, tells you, even if it is strange, unpleasant, grudging or questionable. The author describes cases from politics, criminology as well as abuse and other affectively charged situations, which usually do not end well, because autistic people talk past. What he means, however, is actually the mode of an anticipated truth, a overly hasty conclusion, a verbal relationship naivety. This is exactly the opposite with the psychoanalyst, because he does not believe anything his patient says. Even if the patient does not lie openly, the psychoanalyst still knows that he is definitely not telling the truth. Similar to the clothes salesman, who knows that the other person does not want what he says, but the truth is in the air if you have a good allegory at your disposal. The buyer finally gets a text. . ., a textile.

The psychoanalyst possesses such truth in the form of the 'infantile sexual' discovered by Freud, which remained hidden in the unconscious even late in the life of the neurotic patient. The truth must first be found on the basis of this allegory, because it is still unconscious and can only be clarified through many and long conversations. The psychoanalyst has to lure his patient out of his hiding place by offering 'free association'. Saying whatever comes to his mind reminds the customer in the textile shop, which forces the salesperson to make bold comparisons, and enables the therapist to interpret what is to be decoded from between the lines, between the associations. Now the patient comes to the psychoanalyst in order to find such a clarification that can cure his symptoms, but he resists, he does not want to find the truth immediately and not exactly, he hides inside himself.

In contrast, in Gladwell's descriptions, people do not hide from themselves, but from others, which is particularly clear in the case of the shielding of double agents. A female agent, who was employed as a spy by the American CIA, had to hide from her bosses during the prescribed biannual tests by them, because in reality she was working for the Cuban secret service. But it took twenty years before she was arrested, even though there had been repeated suspicions during her interrogations that she was engaged in counter-espionage. They were also mutually autistic.

One time, the double agent hesitated too long with an answer, another time she was clearly confused. The interviewer had wanted to know, whether something had happened on the way home from her office or whether she had seen someone she knew. She had, but it was one of her Cuban colleagues, whom she of course had to pretend not to know. It was considered an agreed sign to call the central office in Havana. After all, a secret service agent cannot simply be called on the telephone. She couldn't even afford a wink when she saw her colleague.

Nevertheless, it was a huge problem when her own inspector, now an the American one, so decidedly asked her if she had seen anyone on her way home. Such a question does not sound like a pure coincidence, the interviewer must have known everything. He must have known about this distinctive mark, right? Because he could also have asked, "did you get a call from Cuba days ago"? Or "Where were you the day before yesterday?" Anything could be a hoax or the truth. The double agent almost collapsed because of the question about the way home, the colleague from Cuba might have revealed something. But she simply said 'no', they saw nobody and - nothing happened. The interviewer was in the "truth mode " and believed her. The visible associations of her confusion were not used. Only much later was she exposed.

However, the two psychoanalytic autistic people, the therapist and his patient, constantly try to expose themselves, because they have nothing else to say. "There is, however, one thing that makes it possible to break up this autism, and that is that language is a common feature and that is the guarantee that psychoanalysis does not irreducibly limp from what I have just called "autism in pairs".[2] So it is not so bad when two people, total strangers, each with their own individuality, sit down together to express themselves and reveal themselves when they use the common feature, which is the language that opens and reveals itself totally. Of course the double agents do not do exactly that, which is in contradiction to the way it is in psychoanalysis.

But is it really always enough to be able to speak openly to anyone at any time and with anyone, if one so wishes? After all, it could be the case that no one can do anything with the other person's sentence, for example, that the salesperson thinks his customer is crazy. Or the patient in psychoanalysis has a resistance to the Id, not only from his Ego, but from the depths of his Id, of his driving forces, to block the revelations of an 'infantile sexual'. For this reason, that of perfect non-understanding and non-comprehension, the well-known linguist N. Chomsky tried to find a grammatically correct sentence that is meaningless.

Chomsky wanted to show that the essence of language can only be grasped formally and not purely in terms of content. He wanted his generative grammar to be the original formula par excellence, and semantics, i.e. connections of meaning and other things based on it, to be

---

[2] Lacan, J., Seminaire 24 from 19. 4. 1977, translated by R. Nemitz.

developed. The sentence that Chomsky finally found, which was to be completely meaningless in terms of content, read as follows: "Colorless green ideas sleep furiously". Sounds really quite chaotic. Now, this sentence is absolutely not meaningless.

It was perhaps invented at a time when there were no Green parties or corresponding politicians. For the fact that 'green ideas' can be 'colourless' and perhaps even 'sleep terribly' because of this, does not sound - at least psychologically - nonsensical. Politically, one may discuss it or even the opposite may be true. Later, linguists therefore chose a different sentence: "The Gnafel gircht, that Inkeln are schnofel". But here too, there is clearly - perhaps even better than in the first sentence - a sense to be found. The 'Gnafel' may be a somebody, possibly a mythical fairy-tale figure, a goblin or gnome, but in any case he is one who obviously does not speak a modern language. He mumbles, grumbles, grunts, groans, gargles or articulates himself in any other way. Furthermore, it is clearly expressed that the Inkeln (probably similar and yet opposite creatures than the Gnafels, because both names sound like medieval, strange creatures) are 'schnofel' (stupid, shabby, snotty or whatever is meant more derogatory). So the statement of this sentence is clear and not meaningless.

Lacan therefore rightly thinks that every sentence - however disfigured it may be - has meaning. He wanted to point to the meaning of the unconscious, that area of the soul, which - as he says - 'is structured like a language' and thus can articulate itself somehow meaningfully, even if it does not happen by itself. Like a 'language' means: the unconscious is structured in a symbolic order, following a sound-sign order, in such a way that the dimension of logical mediation is completely present, in which - the other way round to Chomsky's theory - truth (and thus of course also lies) can play a decisive role.

For nature, and also sober linguistics, itself knows no truth. There may be terms like 'right' in the sense of appropriate and 'wrong' (negative, non-conforming), but not truth and lie. Even Gladwell's double agent did not lie when she said 'no', because she walked past her colleague as if he did not exist. To have seen something that does not exist - she could answer with 'no'. It would be disastrous for a double agent to lie, he would not be able to get out of the web of lies one day. Between her and her interviewer it was all about right or wrong. Right was being a perfect spy for the Americans. That's what she had to base all her statements on. Her downfall was that she could no longer talk totally past each other.

Later, when the Americans wanted to condemn her to death, she argued credibly that she had only come to spy because she felt sorry for the Cubans who had been bullied by America. That was the truth, but it was no longer, or never, asked. Compassion was neither right nor wrong. And so the secret service, like many scientists today, use - as Lacan continues to say - the 'preformed model of a correct and true answer' - and do not attach importance to the fight for the essence of language and for the fundamental truth'.[3]

They are in the mode of a preformed model of conversation, a fundamental communicative lie, in which it is all about right and wrong, although it is claimed that everyone is looking for the truth. Out of this talking past, this false-right, these not meaningless but worthless sentences, the truth is always circumvented, lied to or completely destroyed. The false right, the 'preformed', is a category in the figurative, in the imaginary, in the image-effecting, while the 'true answer' is a category in the symbolic, in the word-effecting. This is why in this book, with the concept of the 'vertical Ego', I try to create an institution that goes beyond these two categories by combining them in the closest possible way.

Sounds puzzling, but it is about nothing else than when, in the sixties and seventies of the last century, there was fierce debate about whether one could talk to the communists and communicate with them truthfully. Many people said that the Communists only wanted world revolution, and that they would only use a conversation for their own purposes, as a diversion, so to speak, and that the Soviet Union was behind the attack on the West (all this is the pictorial 'preformed'). And indeed, in the Cuban Missile Crisis of 1962, the Russians were about to install missiles that would have reached far into America, but turned back when the President, at the time J. F. Kennedy, threatened with nuclear war, which

---

[3] Lacan, J., Seminar I, Walter (1986) P. 202

was not the most authoritative language either. But peace was maintained, and so it was the right, truthful answer.

But there is a better combination of these basic categories, which will also be important for my further writing. A better combination, in that it can come from within each individual, for which I want to offer here a help to self-help with the 'vertical Ego', which will turn psychoanalysis somewhat the other way round. Lacan pointed out at a later point in time (congress from 7-9 July 1978) that Freud may have "invented a rather bizarre story called the unconscious".[4] And further: "The unconscious is perhaps a Freudian delusion, it explains everything, but like a certain Karl Popper, philosopher, who has well expressed, that it explains too much". Explaining too much always leads to a suggestive substantiation of what is to be said and to exuberant attempts at meaning. Just as in the "Colorless green ideas sleep furiously", where a clear sense is expressed in only five words despite total distortion, the sense is also present in abundance in the unconscious, and one must have a good method to extract the really pictorial and at the same time worthwhile sense. The one where it shows itself, where it reveals itself, and where it speaks of itself and is not just talked about.

At the congress just mentioned, Lacan argued that psychoanalysis was not properly communicable, probably because of the lack of emphasis on the pictorial and the

---

[4] Lacan, J., Congress concerning the transmission of Psychoanalysis from 9. 7. 1978

demonstrating. Psychoanalytic therapies can be carried out, but trained psychoanalysts themselves do not succeed in communicating Freud's pioneering deed in this substance and magnitude anew. "Psychoanalysis is not transmissible. It is quite annoying that every psychoanalyst is forced - because he must be forced - to reinvent psychoanalysis. . . It is necessary. . that every psychoanalyst reinvents how psychoanalysis can continue". This was a strict and very new and modern statement. For usually psychoanalytical training institutes keep their procedures and regulations conservative and as if they were locked in an academic coterie.

One speaks at a high intellectual level, i.e. specialized erected in the vertical, but only under itself, i.e. horizontally constricted. Classic case of a scholar-republic which is too narrowly specialized vertically and horizontally. Classic case of a scholarly republic which is too narrowly specialized vertically and horizontally. But this problem is well known to psychoanalysts. As in the treatment of the sick, the psychoanalyst in didactic analysis should be completely abstinent, i.e. he should not bring anything of his Id, Ego or superego into the conversation scene. "The boundary between the fantasy-relationship and the relationship-reality" must not be uncertain, which is impossible, however, especially in a training institute where the didactic analysis also takes place.[5]

---

[5] Körner, J., The Abstinence of the Didactic Analyst, Journal of Psychosomatic Medicine and Psychoanalysis Nr.2 (1994)

Well, I will try a new invention in this book by pointing out the procedure of *Analytic Psychocatharsis* developed by me and also give a detailed description of it in the appendix. In this process the Ego is not erected in a specialized way, but broadly and thoroughly. Colleagues have told me that my method is very interesting, but not psychoanalysis, and certainly not a further development of it. But that is what happened to Lacan himself when he was excluded from the International Psychoanalytical Society. He was even accused of charlatanry, and in the meantime he has become the most widely received psychoanalyst after Freud. He compared his exclusion with the 'excommunicatio major', the papal, autocratic demonstration of power.

The scholars did not want to be deprived of their dictates of opinion and founded new institutes in ever new school directions, held scholastic congresses and allowed only the 'normopaths' (Bird, 1986), conservative, conformist contemporaries, for psychoanalytic training, and promoted the 'dull normals' (Kernberg, 1984), the 'stinking normals', who essentially had the amenities of the economic and social privileges of the upper middle class in mind".[6] As psychoanalyst Thomä notes, in recent decades doctrinal analysis has been increasingly stylised into superanalysis (supertherapy).[7] In a new issue of the journal PSYCHE this problem of psychoanalytic training institutes is discussed in detail. For it has

---

[6] Cremerius, J., Vom Handwerk des Psychoanalytikers (The craft of the Psychoanalyst), frommann- holzboog (1990)
[7] Thomä, H., Psyche Nr 2 (1992) S. 115 -144

long been known that the procedure for admission to psychoanalytic training is marked by too much bias and prejudice, by opacity and particularism.[8] One has to go to three analysts selected by the Institute, who in the end do not tell you in any way what they think of you. Even at an advanced stage - even after hundreds of hours of teaching analysis and several years of this costly training - there are still cases of refusal to be admitted to the profession of analytical psychotherapist. The psychoanalyst G. Schneider therefore remarks that "it is in any case not inconceivable that ... a candidate takes legal action against his non-admission or failure to pass the final colloquium ...".[9] The union that Freud founded for the benefit of mankind becomes a kind of inquisition.

For all these reasons, attempts are now being made to establish admission and formation criteria with high scientifically defined "categories of candidate competence".[10] Self-awareness and awareness of others, regulation of emotions, conceptualization ability and many other aspects must be present in the candidate in the declaration cited by the author. The fact that one goes to lectures and seminars and completes a teaching analysis is no longer enough. Of course, it can no longer be like in the times of the founder S. Freud. To S. Bernfeld, who was neither a doctor nor a psychologist, Freud said: "When you know what transference and resistance is,

---

[8] Tuckett, D., Does anything go? Towards a framework for the more transparent assessment, Int J Psychoanal 86 (2005)
[9] Schneider, G., PSYCHE Nr. 2 (2020) S. 145
[10] Israelstam, K., PSYCHE Nr. 2 (2020) S. 83 - 117

start to treat". In fact, Bernfeld was then a teaching analyst for thirty years.

But the more intuitive, previous way of determining candidate competence is only further narrowed, censored and overloaded by such a highly intellectualized, multi-layered filtering method as the one mentioned above. The psychoanalyst Heenen-Wolf sees the cause of such regulations in the protracted transference processes.[11] As is well known, the patient transfers to his therapist, but also the finished psychoanalyst transfers to other colleagues, meanings (feelings, impulses, thought contents etc.) from previous or other relationships. These transferences make sense, because interpretations of the motives and mental structures of the transferer can be drawn from them. However, they are mostly imbued with idealizations and personal idiosyncrasies, which ultimately have the same effect as clan formations or the crony clubs mentioned above.

I could not recognize all this at the beginning of my training. I only noticed the schoolmasterly, sometimes bourgeois and petty-minded manner of most of the members of the institute, when I would have wished for personalities radiating sovereignty. Therefore, after my training, I did not join any professsional association from the beginning of my education on. To become a double agency (to stand for psychoanalysis, but also to criticize it) it was enough to practise the profession for a

---

[11] Heenen-Wolf, S., Die psychoanalytische Institution, PSY-CHE Nr. 11 (2016) S. 1077 - 1088

few decades and to have time for other things, such as yoga and meditation.

Well, in this sense I will try to reinvent this book by pointing out the method of *Analytic Psychocatharsis* which I have developed and also give a detailed description of it in the appendix. In this procedure the Ego is not set up in a specialized way, but broadly and comprehensively. Colleagues have told me that my method is very interesting, but not psychoanalysis, and certainly not a further development of it. But that is what happened to Lacan himself when he was excluded from the International Psychoanalytical Society. He was even accused of charlatanry, and in the meantime he has become the most widely received psychoanalyst after Freud. He compared his exclusion with the 'excommunicatio major', the papal, autocratic demonstration of power.

This allowed me to formulate psychoanalysis in a different way, from its flip side, the more pictorial, imaginary side, while it is classically more attached to the worthy, symbolic side. Lacan already titled his seventeenth seminar "The Flip Side of Psychoanalysis", shifting it from its linguistically emphasized side to that of proper names, word games, geometric and topological peculiarities. In a similar manner, I have now, for example, turned the well-known listening "with equal attention" on the part of the analyst around to the side of the analysand, in that in *Analytic Psychocatharsis* it is now the analysand himself who listens with "equal attention". And that means to his own unconscious.

In my method the analysand, in this case the practitioner, the test person, must adopt this basic meditative attitude. As in psychoanalysis, it is a matter of listening half in a trance. However, he must not only listen to himself with "equal attention", he must also do what the psychoanalytic session is all about with "free associations", spontaneous, free ideas. As is well known, in psychoanalysis the patient (or client) brings his transference, i.e. he transfers meanings (feelings, impul-ses, etc.) from previous or other relationships to the therapist, who asks him to say spontaneously and freely whatever comes to his mind.

This is also talking in trance-like impetuosity, from which the therapist can give out his interpretations. Some say: Therapist and patient dream the interpretation together. Similarly, though almost the other way round, the analytical psychocathartic subject must make his unconscious speak, in that it is now responsible for answering with "free associations". A formulation (so-called formula words), which is linguistically completely relevant and yet does not say anything definitively, which the respondent rehearses in his mind, helps to do this. In other words: the unconscious brought into a certain state by the aforementioned formulation plays the role of the therapist here, in that it itself provides the interpretations necessary for the truth of the practicing subject. These interpretations come out in spontaneously heard, mentally 'heard' formulations, which I call *pass-words*.

An example. A long time ago, while practicing *Analytic Psychocatharsis*, I had heard such a *pass-word*: "One must load up men and women". Strange, what does that mean? In my case, I suppose it means patients of both sexes, but what does loading up mean? Loading up with what, or simply loading up oneself with their problems, to containerize them as psychoanalysts like to say? I think it meant both, and with regard to 'loading up with 'what' it immediately came to my mind: with transference. This is especially useful when, for example, in a one-hour setting (one therapy hour only once a week), the transference might subside too quickly or break off completely.

The transference is the supporting thread that runs through the psychoanalytic, but also analytically cathartic treatment and that must not become too loose, too invisible, but at least remain slightly tense. A positive, but also negative transference in the direction of the therapist sets the unconscious in motion, under whose involvement the unconscious can now be freely spoken, 'freely associated' and then interpreted and analyzed. The central element, which lies between associations, free ideas and even dreams and all their interpretations, is the same in both procedures. Lacan calls it a "linguistic crystal", I will explain this in more detail.

I treated many people only in this one-hour setting and always in the same comfortable, slightly reclined sitting position, but maintaining the transmission for six days was not always easy. The same day of the week and the same time of day reinforced the above-mentioned thread a little, but overall it was mostly not entirely satisfactory. When I developed the method of Analytic Psychocatharsis, I came up with the idea of advising some of my clients to use their exercises during the week and combine them with psychoanalytic therapy, so to speak.

The problem was easily solved in this way, but even among the few to whom I could recommend this additional method, some of them were increasingly failing in their efforts to perform the exercises of *Analytic Psychocatharsis* for at least half an hour a day. For most of those who came to Analytical Psychotherapy, however, I could not even offer my method, they did not want to know about it. That was understandable, they had finally come to a fixed agreed upon and paid by the health insurance companies type of therapy, and should now additionally do homework with another, unknown method.

But for myself it was clear that the method of *Analytic Psychocatharsis* was well suited to keep the thread of transmission in tension even longer than a week. With time I came to realize that it could even keep itself tense for months and years. So I had to develop the procedure as something on its own, even if I recommended the combined method here and there. In the completely independent method of *Analytic Psychocatharsis* there is no need to press for an interpretation that is not delayed too long. Like psychoanalyst E. Loibner writes,[12] it must come of its own accord, which is why the physical pres-

---

[12] Loibner, E., Zur Vertiefung der Übertragung (Deepening transference), PSYCHE 1 (2020) S. 26-44

ence of the therapist is only conditionally necessary here. Further details are given in the following.

## 2. Image- and Word-Acting[13]

I do not want to bore the reader with too much abstraction. Admittedly, scientific accuracy and clarity must be guaranteed, but that can also be done in a narrative way. For example, Freud distinguished between three forms of identification, i.e. identifying oneself, experiencing oneself identically. Let me mention two of them first. The first is the one in which one identifies with the male or female around the age of three, the one in which one is already invested from birth. In the case of neurotic development one can also identify with the opposite sex. As is well known, the hysterical-neurotic woman usually appears in a manly manner, uses the theatrically big word and makes erotic allusions, although she does not want the sex she suggests. Similarly, only the other way round, the hysterical-neurotic man.

He wants to be gallant, soft, flexible, playful and witty, but the actor stands out as the feminine hysterical melodramatist. He seems like a queer gay man, although he has nothing to do with homosexuality.[14] Women are supposed to fall in love with the softie, with the charming man, who however often has a problem with his potency, and so it happens to women like Elsa von Brabant with Lohengrin, who was also such a smart guy. Lohengrin, as is well known, forbids asking who he is. He plays with a mystically exaggerated ancestry, and

---

[13] I use this terms synonymously with Lacan's imaginary and symbolic signifiers.

[14] But it is often the shadow image of his neurosis.

typically on his wedding night he can't get around the answer: that he is imposing, but also impotent, and so he fails. The whole thing starts with the fact that Elsa von Brabant only wants a man whom God has chosen! That is schizophrenic! Of course, on the wedding night she had to ask him, 'What's wrong with you?' Then he collapsed and blamed his failure on her.

The second identification in Freud's case is with the father. This means least of all the biological father, but rather the one who conveys the father figure as the guideline giver, as the highest of the clan, the exemplary per se, yes, the extraterritorial, whose father's word is widely accepted. It is about fatherhood, in which the word of the father also comes from the one who is himself the father of the word, who is therefore also the creator of language and discourses. For language was introduced at some point in time, not by the Australopithacei, the pre-humans, but much earlier. It was founded by an intersubjectivity, by a connection or context of subjects that has always existed. Only it was not so explicitly verbal in the beginning, which is why it was placed in a god, which was the best thing to do for thousands of years.

But I want to remain a scientist and I don't have to touch God. Lacan did not do this either and tried to explain what Freud called more mythically than scientifically the "father of prehistoric times" by the primordial Other, that is, by "identification with the real of the real Other.[15] That doesn't sound much more comprehensible ei-

---

[15] Lacan, J., Seminaire XXII from 18. 3. 75

ther, and so there is no need to understand it. I think I communicate it better with the term 'vertical Ego', i.e. a vertical relationship to oneself, in that the usual self has a predominantly horizontal relationship, a relationship from itself to the outside of things and people. The 'vertical Ego', on the other hand, has a relationship to itself primarily but also thoroughly in the two categories mentioned above, in the image-effecting and word-effecting, in the imaginary and the symbolic, in the perception and speech instinct, as Lacan puts it, which I will explain further.

Lacan was quite horrified by the linguist N. Chomsky mentioned at the beginning when he explained to him that for him the linguistic is an organ, a tool![16] According to Chomsky, language is a human tool that can have an effect on man himself, whereas Lacan is of exactly the opposite opinion: 'Man speaks' - has the ability to symbolise - 'but he does so, because the symbol has made him a man'![17] Something symbolic, a primitive symbolic order, a kind of 'legend', 'speech', yes, of an Id Speaks is already there before man appears, i.e. with this Id Speaks (inside and outside of him) he appears fully.

Here, not a god must become active, for "nature provides signifiers," writes Lacan, and with this he also emphasizes the imaginary, the pictorial, the figurative order. "Even before actual human relationships arise,

---

[16] Lacan, J., Le Sintome, Seminaire Nr. XXIII from 9.12.75
[17] Lacan, J., Schriften I, Walter (1980) S. 117

certain conditions are already determined. Even before any experience, before all individual deduction and even before any collective experience . . . there is something that organizes this field and inscribes the first lines of power in it . . the function of a first classification".[18] Lines of power are thus significant signs, supporting phenomena, images that show something, an Id Shows, Id Rays. Something that shows itself already exists, and if the symbolic order has an effect on this seemingly significant thing that shows itself, the radiating lines of power can be called 'imaginary signifiers' as a counterpart to the symbolically ordering, the 'verbal signifiers'. In the beginning, therefore, the Two who are effective in image and word were verbal and imaginary signifiers.[19]

"What is important for us" - Lacan continues - "is that we recognize here the level on which - even before every formation of a subject that thinks - it already counts, on which it is counted. What is important is that in this counted one counting thing is already there".[20] A counting that counts the lines of power, a counting that shows itself, is also already a complex narrative, an Id Rays /

---

[18] The meaning of the signifiers will be explained in the further text and especially on the following pages.

[19] Even though mathematical set theory assumes the three (or majority), principles and powers in science are generally reduced to the two fundamental ones.

[20] Lacan, J., Die vier Grundbegriffe der Psychoanalyse (the four elementary ideas of Psychoanalysis), Walter (1980) S. 26

Id Speaks.[21] There we have it, what mathematicians since Pythagoras have always maintained: Something that really counts, sounds and signs that really apply, an Id Rays and Speaks already existed in pre-human times (and even before that). And exactly this combination of imaginary and symbolic signifiers, which simply counted, made him human (and especially because they were successfully combined).

Not only the large brain made the leap to homo sapiens - the brain certainly was also involved, considering e.g. the Neanderthal brain was even larger than ours. It was also not only the group dynamics that were the cause of special human development, because this also exists in many groups of animals, which nevertheless have not yet become human-like. Nevertheless, this also played a role in the combinations of signifiers. This Id Speaks and Rays in the unconsciousness of every human being, and their combination I emphasize here again.

Even if a so-called language gene (Fox2 gene) exists, each child must learn language from the ground up on its own - mediated by the intersubjective connection/context. Perceptive vision, too, must first be acquired from the interaction of the above-mentioned lines of power. Certainly, the larynx, which has slipped deeper, was essential for the ability to form differentiated sounds, also essential for human speech. But the deci-

---

[21] Intentionally I use here only the pure 3rd person singular, because it is mainly not about man as a thinking subject, but as a subject of the unconscious. And it is not the human being who speaks from his *Ego*, but It speaks in him.

sive thing is the development of phonemes, verbal signifiers, of words, and so in the end it is all about something creative, about 'words of creation', which especially the unconscious brings about when provoked with the *formula-words*.

So the child is the co-creator, even a little father of his own language, he has to learn what language is and how to use it between feelings and drives, between visual and auditory experiences and all the inner and outer influences. The unconscious plays an important role in this, not only because much is repressed there early on, also in linguistic form, but also because the prelexive physical rests there in the form of the aforementioned lines of power, the manifestation of the imaginary signifiers from earliest intersubjectivity. The unconscious is the language of the Other to be written in capital letters, but also the image of the auratic 'Ding' (the thang), as Lacan calls it.[22]

| image-effecting | word-effecting |
|---|---|
| imaginary signifier | verbal signifier |
| Id Rays | Id Speaks |
| looking drive | speaking drive |
| 'Ding' (the thang) | the Other |

In order to avoid the confusion of the terms I use all the time, I am putting a small scheme into the text here, which should give some overview of the two basic cate-

---

[22]Lacan called it always with its German name, so do I here.

gories, as they are already used, but will also be further supplemented below. Diversity is necessary because it repeatedly highlights a different aspect. Thus, L'Autre, the significant Other, is not only an inner partner in dialogue derived from the significant figures.[23] The same is true for the auratic 'Ding' that comes from the earliest self-mirrorings, body-self-mirrorings, and represents the imaginary, iconic side of the unconscious that can hardly ever be described. None of these signifiers have a clear meaning on its own, only their combination makes the decisive sense. I make use of this fact in *Analytic Psychocatharsis*, because this original connection was not used so extensively by classical psychoanalysis. The not quite vertical line between the two categories of the illustration should already indicate the position of the 'vertical Ego'.

But what are signifiers anyway? The philosopher Byung-Chul Han calls them signs of excess, even of what is luxurious in meaning. "Only the excess, the surplus of the signifier makes language appear magical, poetic and seductive. . Signifiers enter into neighbourly relationships without regard for the signified", for the soberly redefined signified. All this concerns the verbal signifier, the word-effecting, while the 'neighbourly' refers to the lines of power of the imaginary signifier,

---

[23]The Other represents the internalization of parents, teachers, superiors, psychoanalysts etc. and their laws in the form of *Ego*-ideal, superego, and other things. The O is also written as a crossed out O, because this mental, linguistic instance is not a guarantor of truth.

which is even more luxurious, kaleidoscopically dazzling and seductive.

One can well illustrate these facts again with the double agent, because what - apart from earning money - does he actually want? The above-mentioned double agent working for America and Cuba said she wanted to help poorer Cuba, but the argument sounded weak. The signifiers in the background, herself unconsciously, say something else. They murmur something of recognition, mysteriously suggest something exciting, glamorous, foaming at the mouth in a game of risk, of life and death. The signifiers combine inner and outer in a beguiling way. "Mysterious is not the signifier" (here the term double agent), "but the signifier without the signified", Byung-Chul Han continues to write. This means that the abundance and the foaming of the signifier have turned into the delirious, into the adventurous chaotic. It can no longer be found in any signifier; it correlates with the infantile drive objects, unconscious phantasms that psychoanalysts filter out of "free associations" and dreams of their patients. The double agent would have been better off in therapy in time.

Because she does not know her "Ding", does not know the thing she is doing. It is only something objective, a thing, albeit a dangerous thing. Lacan's 'Ding' is close to the imaginary and I will go into this in more detail. For the time being, once again briefly to the Other. For the double agent he incarnates exactly in the interviewer who is supposed to check and control her, but he is stuck in his "truth mode". He is blocked, inhibited, castrated, as they say in psychoanalysis, he ∤s O, and so he cannot do anything for the real truth (in the negative: he cannot expose her, in the positive: he is not the one who could enlighten her about the glamorous, infantile and breakneck. He is unfortunately not a therapist).

In *Analytic Psychocatharsis* the therapist, who is himself a representative of this Other, is excluded as a physically existing listener, but he is replaced by the fact that one listens directly to one's own unconscious. This is how real truth comes to light. Listening is fundamentally important in psychoanalysis, even if the therapist should not give an immediate answer to what he hears. The less he says, the better. A computer program that is supposed to know more than you know yourself can also have this effect. One insinuates that someone is with you by being a nobody equipped with the ability to speak. In *Analytic Psychocatharsis* it is the other way round. Here one has to call the nobody with the *formula-words*, even provoke him, in order to hear his answer, which corresponds to the analyst's interpretation.

The procedure of *Analytic Psychocatharsis* contains analytical and psychological-meditative foundations; it uses not only "evenly suspended attention" but also Freud's statement on "free association". The patient on the couch should say everything that comes to his mind spontaneously, as freely and uninfluenced by embarrassing or rational thoughts as possible. This never succeeds completely or optimally. Similarly in *Analytic Psychocatharsis*, where personal and logical associations should be added to the thoughts emerging from the unconscious in order to interpret the "free associations" mentioned. Analogous to the *formula-words*, I call the then finally formulated thoughts Pass- or Identity-Words, because they have to do with the truth of the practitioner and his further development. More on this later.

And why is there not also the mother of the word? After all, we speak in our mother tongue first and for all our lives. But the mother tongue could almost be a language without words. All people quickly associate the same thing with mother: to care for, nurture, nourish, warm and certainly also exchange binding gestures and signs. Psychoanalysts, however, believe that first the word of the father from the Oedipus myth as well as from the myths of the neurotics and now especially the word "do not touch the mother" directed to the son, changed everything and revealed the creative power of the word. A certain commanding tone, words of power, play a role here.

Lacan thinks that the idea of the verbal signifier, the word-actor, is typical for the male-fatherly side, which means that it emphasizes particularly strongly the relation to meaning, while the female-maternal side contains more communicative elements in the direction of the above-mentioned pictorial associations.[24] Simplified: women talk confidentially, engagingly, pictorially mediating, men only get to the point. While the imaginary signifier of the amorous-erotic is equivalent in both sex-

---

[24] Lacan, J., Seminar XXIII, Das Sinthom, Turia & Kant, (2017) S. 118

es,[25] the linguistic, the verbal signifier, is weighted differently.

The counterpart of this male-fatherly word creation "Don't eat your little ones ", which is directed at the mother and spouse, also has this distinctive significance in psychoanalysis. In the Oedipus myth it is represented by the sphinx, which eats up anyone who does not solve its riddle. However, someone like the Sphinx does not listen to such admonishing and forbidding words. Oedipus had to solve the riddle first, he couldn't just succeed with one command. He had to appease the animal in the woman and the woman in the animal, just as the kiss and embrace of the prince in Grimms' fairy tales always does.

And so Oedipus, when asked by the Sphinx what moves four limbs in the morning, two at noon and three in the evening, says that this is the trinity of human beings: child, woman and man, whose third limb is not difficult to guess. It is exactly the same thing that a woman once betrayed when she expressed a well-known metaphor for letting oneself go and being relaxed in this way: "Today I want to let all five straight". Five? Big laughter, she didn't want to let the fifth one be straight, just the other way round, like the sphinx, she just wanted to have her peace from this superfluous limb.

Usually the riddle of the sphinx is interpreted in such a way that one should see the old man's stick in the third

---

[25] According to Freud this is the so-called 'phallic phase', which is equivalent for both sexes (more later)

limb or leg. But - to be honest - isn't that the version told to children? Such a huge, animalistic, feminine figure doesn't give you such a shallow philistine riddle, there's more to it than that. It's a bit about stepping out of the horizontal into the vertical, even if it's not yet the finished 'vertical Ego'. Lacan would call the separating / connecting line in the illustration (page 27) as well as in the illustration of the painter G. Moreau standing next to here, which shows Oedipus and the Sphinx with a clear emphasis on the vertical, the real. For as the philosopher C. Rosset noted, one only comes close to the real when one agrees with one's doubles - i.e. the two basic categories mentioned above - and this is only possible with the help of the 'vertical Ego'.[26] On the left of the picture the sphinx with its lion's body conveys the perfect picture-effect, the puzzle-solving Oedipus the word-effect, combined in their common vertical.

The human being with the third limb has in antiquity as a tripod, ancient Greek. τρίπους trípous, also has cultic meaning, for example in Delphi. It also symbolizes the female sex, which could give the riddle of the sphinx a

---

[26] Rosset, C., Das Reale, Traktat über die Idiotie (The Real, Treatise on Idiocy), Suhrkamp (1988) S. 50-63

very strict meaning.[27] Perhaps Oedipus should have answered the question about man with the τρίπους, the third limb, with the answer to the question 'What does it mean to be a woman'. But he would have failed, he would have answered with excuses, and even in Iokastes bed he would have been more the child in their arms than the ἐροώμενος, the love artist. He should have answered with his 'vertical Ego'.

This generally addresses the relationship between the sexes, between man and woman, whether the two are defined more socially or more biologically. If one wants to reduce what has just been discussed to an extreme position, one could say for the man that such a position consists in his fixation on the 'phallus' (real, symbolic, imaginary). Lacan once expressed this very drastically when he stated: The man is married to his phallus, he has no other wife. This hefty statement concerns, as already mentioned, an extreme position that could be like this on the side of the woman: The woman is fixated on her baby's cuddling, snuggling and hugging, she doesn't have any other sex. Sounds crass, but the sphinx has that in mind too.

Because, as emphasized once again, the extreme positions are unconscious, only rarely are they almost lived in a kind of perversion or ghost through the myths like that of the sphinx, which has a male lower body and is a pre-oedipal mother-female figure. The being that walks on four legs in the riddle of the sphinx fits well with the mentioned baby, and that which walks on three legs fits

---

[27] Wikipedia: Dreifuß (tripod)

just as well with the mentioned phallus-centered man. And finally, the being that walks on only two legs is like the mature adult, the dispositive man who uses his reason and foresight in life. This is where everyone should go.

Dispositive means that you have to manage the two basic categories with a better combination. By the way, you could have added the word 'truth mode' on the right side of the picture (page 24) and 'picture or pointing mode' on the left. The people described by Gladwell were ok in the linguistic, in the verbal signifier despite talking past each other, but a combination with the directly pictorial, directly pointing, they had not succeeded. The double agent was the Sphinx herself. For as I said, the signifiers alone have no meaning, only in their combination do they become effective.

In the present text, however, it is only a matter of combining the imaginary with the symbolic (verbal). Much more than the symbolic (important for psychoanalysis), the imaginary signifiers (important for *Analytic Psychocatharsis*) are repressed. Therefore it is recommended to dissolve the whole from the last. We already know Oedipus enough, now we just need to know and be able to say clearly who and what the sphinx is and why it symbolizes woman better than the boring pop icons of today.

## 3. The Thing as such

Of course the Sphinx was not Lacan's auratic Ding'.
More on this later. But I wouldn't have to express myself in such a complicated way, because this book is
about a psychic procedure, which I can describe in a
few lines. It combines methods that are believed to be
completely contradictory, such as psychoanalysis and
meditation. The *formula-words* already mentioned are
circular formulations that contain several meanings in a
single line of writing. If one meditates on them, one
cannot prefer any of the meanings and certainly not hear
a common, collective meaning. They are too disparate
for that. For psychoanalysis, too, they are the core of
their theory, because the unconscious is constructed in
the same way. But without having to create extravagant
framework stories around them, hardly anyone would
get anywhere with these few lines.

So I return to the myths of the sphinx, in which, as in
the obscene jokes of men and in Freudian psychoanalysis, women do not come off well. Freud has been accused that his theory of a generalized sexual is still
overly masculine. Yet there were so many young wom-
en in his therapy, so much has changed and so today we
adore the young pop icons, the sexist actresses, rappers
and queer female authors who have emancipated themselves. In a review of Sally Rooney's current bestseller
'Conversations with Friends', Caroline Würfel writes
that the author is described as the "J.D. Salinger of the
Snapchat generation" because she represents the ideal of
female masquerade and writes about passionate sex in

such a way "that you want to have it yourself".[28] Rooney is stylized into hype just because she makes young people talk about everything, including lesbians, transgender, drugs and sadism. The dialogues are flippant, cool and impertinent, everything is offered.

It is therefore about the relationship between man and woman, and about the women, who usually get the short end of the stick. Women therefore usually don't know or appreciate enough of their own immanent enjoyment. I refer to the writings of J. Lacan, who stressed on every third page that the sexual relationship does not really exist anyway, because none of this can be verified, clearly and logically said, or even 'quantified', i.e. cannot be expressed in units of sexual enjoyment. This may seem bizarre, but what does Caroline Würfel really want, what does she mean by "damn good sex", which she herself wants to have right away, as she writes? She sets a measurement which goes down from 'damn good' to medium to probably 'grotty bad'.

To the psychoanalyst, this is not precise enough. After all, many patients come to a psychoanalytical consultation who are already complaining that they don't know how many times a week, a month or a year you have to have sex to be normal. Such a thing, namely a pure count of frequencies, is now actually a bad, cold, mechanical measurement. But since Freud said that boys and girls go through the same "phallic phase" in childhood, that is, that the phallic is the same unit of measurement for both, everything seemed to be clear. There

---

[28] Würfel, C., ZEIT online, Ausgabe 30 (2019)

is equivalence in this respect, mathematical equality, so to speak. Sex does have a certain masculine emphasis, but all this does not change the fact that the phallic is thus a better unit of measurement than the "damn good" or not good, as Mrs. Würfel said?

It is probably a matter of judgement whether other metaphors, picture-word-actings, can be counted in addition to the sexual reviewer's metaphor of the phallic. The excessive emphasis on the phallic, abbreviated with the Greek letter $\Phi$, (Phi), as it is common in psychoanalysis, can be considered a unit of measurement, but you won't get far with it. But psychoanalysts need $\Phi$ to make the therapeutic dialogue provocative, effective and quantified. For it is above all about the infantile-sexual, which is so unconscious and plays an essential role in therapeutic interpretation.

Admittedly, $\Phi$ is not a sufficient signifier for all areas of life and understanding of the world, nothing sufficient in general to have an image-word-acting. But it calls up the infantile forms of eroticism that are at stake and allows them to be integrated, classified and inscribed into other forms, when it is a matter of exposing the lies of human life with an instrument, a signifier, which has no signified. So it cannot be nailed down to one thing, but must be pointed to its ultimately erotic origin, in order to be able to give the whole thing its name in its own language. For it is this naming, blessing, that verticalizes the soul.

In order to clarify all this I would like to start again briefly from the beginning and commence directly from nature, i.e. from the term nature as I have already quoted it at the beginning and as everybody understands it superficially: going out into a landscape, into the green, where flora and fauna prevail, pure nature so to speak including the people. That is a very comprehensive approach for acquiring a general orientation, isn't it? Biology, zoology, anthropology, but also social sciences, knowledge about how the brain works and many other scientifically founded things should be included here and be sufficient to answer the question: Can this nature tell me the truth? The truth about me and the world? The truth that underlies everything?

For knowledge alone is not enough. Psychoanalysts assume that it is not being, something, even the Kantian 'thing as such' that is the cause of everything, but the truth behind it. They start from the symptom, not only from the symptom of the illness, but also from the fact that so much, if not everything, is only symptomatic, and that behind the symptom are not things, but truths. If one uncovers the truth in analytical psychotherapy, the symptom disappears and a certain awareness of the connections arises.

Now this kind of truth-finding is not applicable to everything. Psychoanalysis is much too much dominated by language and speech, and thus by linguistics. It moves mainly in the area of verbal signifiers and leaves out the second area, that of the imaginary signifier. After all, it has created an important concept, that of libido, the energy of desire, longing, demands, drives. Even though Freud primarily used libido to make his sexual theory work, he also mentions several times a "desexualized libido", which usually has something to do with the sublimation of all these forms of desire. Is libido therefore a universal energy?

Yes, and no. Libido probably remains something very bound to human existence. Do plants also have libido? No, even with animals one has to ask oneself whether they know of such a thing, because with theirs we are talking mainly about the instincts that regulate the field of the significant forces. Instincts are hormonal, neuro-controlled, and this control is relatively narrow, rigid. Also the triggers for instinctive behaviour, e.g. for mating behaviour, are strictly correlated, acting like an inside-to-outside image mechanism. The decisive discovery of the behavioural scientist K. Lorenz was to have proved that animals are, however, capable of developing new instincts within this rigid framework of the picture-to-picture correspondence (pure imaginary signifiers) of their instincts/drives for self-preservation and species survival. There are always processes in animals in which the instinct is briefly abandoned in favour of the freedom of desire that is otherwise only common in humans. The best example is the dead-man's reflex, which appeared late in the animal kingdom. In a state of highest tension, it must have come to an instinct exit, which made a flash of inspiration possible, but which then solidified again as instinct.

The question whether nature can tell the truth, but also whether libido is something comprehensively substantial, thus remains unanswered. But now there must already be something in the plant world that can do without the help of libido, at least where there is asexual reproduction (apomixis and horizontal gene transfer). If one further assumes that "the universe is the sum of all signifiers" as Lacan states, in the plant kingdom the picture-to-picture proportion, the proliferation of the imaginary signifiers rather than the determining one, is valid. It is even more decisive than it already is in the animal kingdom. But what then represents the libido in flora?

In the plant kingdom too, there is enjoyment, as Lacan says - he also assures us that the trees, the amoebae and bacteria enjoy it.[29] "The very fabric of all forms of enjoyment borders on the body, and that is the dress by which one recognizes it - if a plant were not obviously suffering, we would not know it were alive".[30] Lacan also discusses elsewhere the enjoyment of the plant world from a form similar to the unconscious.[31] I call this most original enjoyment, which is inherent in flora itself, 'autochthonous', and it seems to be so elementary and original that people have largely suppressed, forgotten or rejected it. One gets closer to it, if, as already mentioned, one meditates in a secure way, based on the science of psychoanalysis, and if one has a strong cathartic experience. One must understand it as a science f r o m the subject.

---

[29] Lacan, J., Seminar XXI, lecture from 23. 4. 1974.

[30] Lacan, J., Seminar XVIII, lecture from 17. 3. 1971

[31] Lacan, J., Lettres de L'Ècole freudienne, Nr. 16 (1975) S. 192

I want to distinguish myself from esoteric attempts, which only intuitively and almost magically speak of the 'secret life' of plants. P. Wohlleben, who writes here with his books about the 'secret life of trees and nature', is certainly right when he attributes a certain consciousness, complex communication and sensations to plants, but he also creates strong misunderstandings of a conceptual kind. Concerning the plants, all is about something purely reflective, a blind mirroring. The biologist C. Ammer writes that, in contrast to Wohlleben's ideas of analogies social interaction among plants and trees, there is blatant competition among all these plants. Every trunk fights for its survival. Trees would also react to sound waves without being able to "hear" as Wohlleben claims.[32]

And U. Schraml, Professor of Forestry and Environmental Policy, therefore believes that Wohlleben glides from metaphor to metaphysics. He starts from similarities, which have nothing to do with real science. Wohlleben attributes great intelligence to crows, for example, that they are capable of conscious deception. "They lead lifelong relationships. When their females are close, they demonstratively drive away competitors. But when the female is away, any crow that comes near them is sexually assaulted." Well, is that intelligence or drive, maybe both? After all, it's something known to man without much intelligence.

---

[32] Charisius, H., Im Märchenwald (in the fairytale woods), SZ vom 22. 1.2020, S. 14

Our environment lives much more authentically than we see it, yet the life of an amoeba is something different than that of a human being. I have illustrated this in the following figure. There is a horizontal and a vertical axis of the term life. I have illustrated this in the following figure. The vertical x-axis is the one that starts at the bottom with the prokaryotes, cells without a nucleus, viruses, prions. Perhaps one could start with even more undifferentiated forms, that is, with the pure imaginary signifiers. Upward, complexity increases all the way to the human being. The horizontal y-axis is that of the meaning, the symbolic, the verbal signifiers. On the left is the simplest imaginable ecosystem, the relationship between water, air and earth, something similar to the myths of the four elements, but today we count more basic elements.

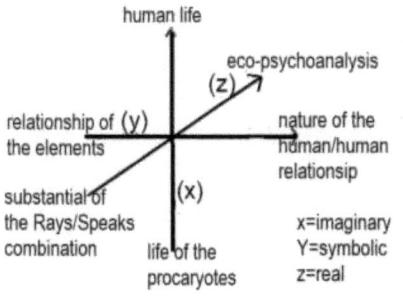

On the far right is the relationship of man to man (I assume that this is the nature of man per se). The z-axis shows what has been called eco-psychoanalysis, which runs diagonally up and down the right side of the whole life and ecosystem, including psychoanalytic basics. It includes the human-human relationship, but only at the outermost edge, just as it hardly deals with the relationships of early forms of "primitive" life. A gardener can be a good eco-psychoanalyst if he or she not only understands botany, but also garden design and even the secrets with which a rare plant, a newly discovered herbal remedy, a particularly aesthetic plant can convey harmony and understanding for all life. But what is the starting point of the z-axis?

Philosophers and ethicists have been asking themselves these questions in their own way for many years. A. Kallhoff, for example, has designed details of a 'plant ethic' that is oriented towards the flourishing of plants and the relationship between man and plant. She assigns a moral status to plants and justifies this, among other things, with the 'objective value of the self-care of the living'. I cannot list here all her very complex ethical-philosophical thoughts. But it is clear that plants have a right of their own to survive, which is often very difficult to convey to the people living with them. The question of morality is therefore difficult to pose, as it is not even considered from a conventional point of view. But - according to Kallhoff - it can be extremely suitable for ethical discussion.

I think that it is even more suitable for clarifying the essence of enjoyment in its multi-layered sense. Again the same scheme, but now in the sense of this text. First to the man / woman relationship. "The sexual relationship", writes Lacan, "is not graspable in its structure",[33] not meaningful, not logically definable nor even "quantifiable". Their relationship is dominated by the emphatically verbal, phallic signifier (the 'plaisir phallique' is only the external Freudian slip of the so-called act of love). And so one has to distinguish the actual enjoy-

---

[33] Lacan, J., Radiophonie, Silicet 2-3:455-99 (1970)

ment, the 'jouissance', from the all too human 'plaisir' and raise it vertically "to the dignity of the 'thing'".[34]

This dignity is reflected in the relationship between human and human, which is to be understood as a horizontal one and which cannot be defined much better than that between man and woman. Sociological, political, economic, family, cultural, national language and other horizontal relationships are in constant flux, get mixed up, enter into cooperation, etc. There is no ultimate reliance on them, they are more likely to be a constant 'forwards failure', the counterpart to the failure of the often so highly acclaimed act of love, which corresponds more to a constant 'being thrown back'.

The only way out is the diagonal. If I emphasize the vertical in this book, it is because it is just as neglected as the horizontal, but I don't want to write a book about social sciences with the goal of how one could finally make everything better. How to avoid wars, how to finally eliminate social injustices, or how to eliminate

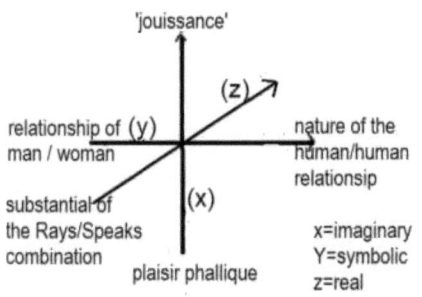

and solve the aforementioned 'forward failure' in the

---

[34] Lacan thinks that the sexual act usually goes wrong and is a fluff, because the man ejaculates at the peak of his anxiety, where he doesn't know what to do.

horizontal. The shelves in bookstores are already full of it, and I don't need to add a new work. My aim here is to clarify and improve the vertical, because then one can end up with the substance of the successful Rays/Speaks combination, whose diagonal aim is now that of every individual who tries to achieve it with *Analytic Psychocatharsis*.

So it is about the 'thing' of the 'jouissance', which I can call autochthonous, auratic or female as many authors have done. For example, psychoanalyst R. Golan, who has defined this feminine of the 'jouissance' as original-libidinous and has worked it out particularly well. The female form of enjoyment, she writes, includes pain and suffering, "but also includes universality, height, boundlessness, knowledge/enlightenment, knowledge, freedom and bliss.[35] So here we come closer to the answer to the question of what is autochthonous enjoyment or 'Jouissance' per se. It does not necessarily have to be a 'fusion' or a 'vision', as Christian mystics have so well demonstrated. But perhaps it has something to do with the substance of the Rays/Speaks complex and the enjoyment of the lowest forms of life, such as plants. For it is, after all, an enjoyment without an object-like background, without an object of love, so to speak, without a purpose just in the middle of the Real.

This is the reason why Lacan ascribes the enjoyment of the real to mathematicians, because they also do not adhere to representational, factual objects, but to numbers. To this day there is no empirically proven theory of the

---

[35] Golan, R. Loving Psychoanalysis, Karnak (2006)

first integers, and so the mathematical construct seems to hang in the air. The most impressive thing about mathematics, however, is the intensity of its verticals, even if they often seem a little out of touch with life. In this respect it sounds contradictory that only the number jugglers are responsible for the final 'jouissance'. Lacan later said quite clearly, that the ultimate 'jouisance' is to be found beyond all other areas of enjoyment.[36]

A unit of measurement for the 'Ding' and the 'jouissance' does not exist and in comparison with $\Phi$ there is no such direct, immediate counterpart on the female side, no complete and precise correspondence. This has a little to do with the fact that women usually underestimate their own enjoyment (Lacan's 'jouissance'), do not give it such great weight and do not put it sufficiently well into a special logical-practical form. They themselves do not believe in it so much or "they lack something of the symbolic material", as Lacan remarked smugly. Well, I don't think you can say it like that. They rather lack what we all lack, namely how to bring together $\Phi$ and its fellow and counterpart, which must exist somewhere and somehow, in a successful, fitting, ideal form. Because the men lack the pictorially psychic, a more stable imaginary order or a better controlled image-effective, body-internal-mirroring, as I would call it.

Elsewhere I have spoken about the feminine of $\Psi$ (Greek Psi) to follow the myth of the god Eros ($\Phi$) and

---

[36] Lacan, J., Seminar XXI, lecture from 12. 3. 1974

the king's daughter Psyche ($\Psi$). But Lacan also speaks in this context of the 'Ding', which is said to be something primordial, already prehistorically effective, the power of a forefather or ancestor, which is active in the psyche of even the most serious human being. So I equated $\Psi$ with the 'Ding' in order to stick to the scientific language of psychoanalysis. "The difference between the 'Ding' and the object or 'la chose'," writes Lacan, "is that the 'Ding' is fundamentally alien, ... in any case is the first outside to which the whole path of the subject is oriented towards. It is without doubt a path of reference, in relation to ... what? To the world of his desires".[37]

I interpret this as follows: we desire too many objects, we are too much object-related, and so we stay low with the phallic 'object', overly grounded, instead of - as Lacan continues - "raising the 'object' to the dignity of the 'Ding'". This means that one has to spiritualize, refine, sublimate oneself to a high degree, in short, and as I want to convey it: verticalize, in order to get to the real of the 'Ding', which is then something completely different than as the oral object for example, which is eaten in the tickle of the palate. Or the sexual object, the phallic body of the woman. Or the object of the gaze, the frivolous curiosity on TV, smartphone, etc.

Lacan's 'Ding' was a homage to Kant and Freud. I will say more about the 'Ding'. For it could be related to the sublimated enjoyment that Lacan claims is female and women themselves would not take it so seriously, would

---

[37] Lacan, J., Seminar VII, Quadriga (1996) S. 66

not appreciate it so much and would repress it. In the phallic phase they would then be taken by surprise and believe that they could find it with Φ, with male affection, sovereignty or even love, as well as successful motherhood. Even as an artist, poet and in all professions, women could get the same, adoration and social recognition, and yet there is still something left open in the calculation of this true and sublimated enjoyment. Because men enjoy two things, social recognition (if they do it right at work) and then there is Φ, the 'plaisir phallique', which women are also entitled to, but only around the male corner, not directly, not true like it is in the 'jouissance'.

So if it is the case, that Φ communicates the unconscious sexual, the erotic metaphor par excellence, and the Other, capital O, is only castrated in us as O with a horizontal line, and the 'Ding' dwells in the mysterious, what is left in psychoanalysis in terms of joy and happiness, in bliss and positive certainty? For at least the Eros life instinct in Freud's work also brings with it the death instinct, an instinct for destruction and annihilation. The literary scholar, E. Goebel, said in general, that Freud, at the latest with the discovery of this destructive or death instinct, screwed up the concept of very own enjoyment in the form of extensive sublimation (especially self-sublimation).[38] "If the striving for deconstruction and death is indeed a drive, active and dynamic, then such a

---

[38] Goebel, E., Jenseits des Unbehagens (Beyond the discomfort), transcript (2009) S. 10 - 14

concept with other alloyed drives of eroticism and death forces too much renunciation and asceticism and leads to pessimism", he writes. There is then no more room for refinement, sublimation and verticalisation, up to and including enjoyment as such, to 'jouissance' and the 'Ding'.

Anyway, Lacan says that psychoanalysis is the "negative of religion", that the religious or 'spiritual', self-sublimated represents the positive, which does not mean that it is better and that Lacan recommends 'spirituality'. "Negative of religion" means that the religious or so-called 'spiritual', soulful path is another side, an opposite side to psychoanalysis, which however is mythical and not scientific. In order to define more precisely the relationship between the 'spiritual' and psychoanalysis, Lacan uses its tripartite division into the symbolic (linguistic), the imaginary (pictorial) and the real (geometric-mathematical).

He has represented this general systematization by the aforementioned three areas in a knotting or grinding, which he calls the Borromean knot. The figure below shows this structure in which three rings are intertwined in such a way, that the three areas overlap, thus making the connections between these three areas clear. It is also visible, that when cutting through only one of the rings, all of them become free. Thus Lacan defines religion as the symbolic realisation of the imaginary, abbreviated RSI, which gives the aforementioned division into three parts a certain direction. This consists in the fact, that something image-effective, imaginary in the sense of the spiritual is realized through language (e.g. the language of the Bible), becomes inwardly real experienceable.[39]

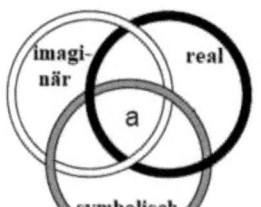

And so psychoanalysis - Lacan continues - would consist, on the other hand, in symbolizing the real imaginary (SRI). As mentioned above, the psychoanalyst does not respond directly to what his client, patient, says, but interposes something in between, namely the unconscious as Freud explored it. The real that is suppressed in the unconscious is expressed linguistically by means of the pictorial-imaginary, by means of conceptions.[40] It is clear that Lacan thus confirms that psychoanalysis cannot be evaluated further and more comprehensively than religion, which of course, in its sublimations as well as in psychoanalysis, does not reach the regions of the 'jouissance'. However, I would like to get there and therefore propose a third way with Analytical Psychoanalysis, which I will shortly call and explain as IRS (imagining the symbolic real). Lacan claims that mathematicians do this.

But there is also a more practical way of IRS than mathematics with its distance to life can do. In their book

---

[39] God as something essentially pictorial, is thus realized in words.

[40] The opposite is true of the psychotic. He realizes the imaginary so intensively that he can only symbolize it in fragments according to the rushing flood of images (RIS).

'Zen Buddhism and Psychoanalysis', D. T. Suzuki, as a connoisseur of Eastern meditation, and E. Fromm as a psychoanalyst have already made a similar attempt. In a profound comparison they try to show that the 'spiritual' and the psychoanalytical are completely equal and that further conclusions can be drawn from them. In the end, however, they have not found any overarching binding result.[41] While Suzuki explains his Zen meditation in sweeping terms (which one readily concedes to the East) and in the paradoxes typical of Zen, Fromm argues just as sweepingly, but at the same time academically detachedly, about his 'humanistic psychoanalysis' (which one cannot concede to the West). Other authors have taken a similar approach, such as B. S. Goel,[42] psychoanalyst R. Zwiebel[43] or H. Stein.[44] But they too have not offered a theoretical and practical solution as a third way.

In fact, it seems to be very difficult to relate meditative-spiritual methods to psychoanalysis in such a way that a constructive result can be achieved. And yet this is possible precisely with the aforementioned three-way division of the IRS, i.e. to imagine the symbolic real. If religion makes the image of God really experiencable through the language of the Bible, it also uses the vertical, but not in the sense of its own psychological be-

---

[41] Suzuki, D. T., Fromm, E., Zen - Buddhismus und Psychoanalyse, suhrkamp (1972)

[42] Goel, B. S. Meditation und Psychoanalyse, Ariston (1989

[43] Zwiebel, R., Weischede, G., Neurose und Erleuchtung, Klett-Cotta (2009)

[44] Stein, H., Freud spirituell, Königstein-Urania Verlag (2001)

ing.[45] With mathematicians now it looks as if there is a clear statement (symbolic) in the arithmetic universe, which the mathematician only has to make clear in reality with his signs (imaginary). The vertical appears too short or too abstract.

I will therefore also choose IRS for *Analytic Psychocatharsis*, because, as I will show, this also applies to this method. It is not numbers that are found, but the 'Ding', even if I feel almost sacrilegious. Because if I present the psychoanalysts as clubmasters who have fallen back into scholasticism and the 'spiritual', the soulful as theoretically and practically incompetent, the mathematicians as too abstract to be able to solve all the problems from the thicket of unconscious desires (the objects of desire), of appropriate sublimations and the combinations of Lacan's sophisticated knots of the symbolic, the real and the imaginary, don't I have to be an impostor, a delusional sacrilegious person, an addict of prestige? But many of those who have been accused of this have turned out to be simple people after all.

---

[45]E. Fromm as a psychoanalyst has already made a similar attempt. In a profound comparison he tries to show that the 'spiritual' and the psychoanalytical are completely equal

## 4. The negative Space

The Hungarian art theoretician and literary critic, L. F. Földényi, sees the concept of melancholy in a positive way. He does not want to understand it as a 'loss of psychic objects' like Freud, but as a metaphysical feeling with which one can work creatively and make good experiences.[46] But Freud used the term more in the sense of a depressive mood, even a psychotic illness. The psychic 'object' that has filled the inner being in its entire being (for example the introject of the so-called 'early mother') has been lost, can no longer be held in soul. It has changed back to an identification, self and 'object' are no longer separate, and thus united in deadly love.

But Földényi chooses the painting of A. Dürer's 'Melancholia' to explain his ideas in this regard, which I will post on the next page for better understanding. It shows a seated angel pondering in front of himself, as one might assume: melancholically pondering in front of himself. His left arm is supported on his knee and holding a compass in his right hand, as if one could measure his state of mind. It is certainly not the absorption due to Freud's 'loss of objects', although one cannot entirely rule out the possibility that Dürer himself was thinking of a so-called 'depressive episode', as the international classification of mental illness (cold catalogued) puts it. But the details of a medical and also psychoanalytical

---

[46]Földényi, L. F., Lob der Melancholie (praise of melancholy), Matthes & Seitz (2019)

nature are not at issue here - especially in relation to Földényi's description. In addition to the many objects and designs, Földényi is primarily concerned with the polyhedron, which is large in the picture on the left and probably cut and polished from stone, which - according to the author - would show that Dürer thus "has given evidence of a very intimate knowledge of melancholy".

"This block of stone is not only a symbol, but also a vividly pulsating expression of melancholy. By entering the space of the painting, this stone block obstructs the view, but again does not obstruct it. And this applies not only to the view, but also to the interpretation of the picture as a whole. . . But no one has yet succeeded in a satisfactory interpretation and unravelling of the stone block". Földényi continues, "the renewal of geometric representations of the time may have contributed to Dürer's introduction of such a polyhedron into the picture. In terms of aesthetics, one could also "speak of the polyhedron as a liberating sight", of avant-garde art, of a play with strangeness and inexplicability. It is as if one had to penetrate the polyhedron by then entering a "negative space", concludes Földéniy.

Negative space? Such a thing applies exactly to every form of successful meditation. One looks for a quiet, calm place, closes one's eyes and signs out. Somehow the feeling of the body image and the sense of space disappears. In the horizontal, to the sides, there is no hold. That is where the images, memories, thoughts come from, which are not important but extensive. Nevertheless, one has to face them. In psychoanalysis it is necessary to reveal oneself before someone else, to admit something, in meditation or *Analytic Psychocatharsis* the revelation takes place through the words of identity or *pass-words*, which make one confess. This is how the vertical straightens up.

In the further course of his book, however, Földényi comes up with the idea that in Stanley Kubrick's famous film 2001: Odyssey in Space, a cuboid block of stone or metal like this plays a decisive role! It appears at turning points in human history, disappears again and appears at the end like a memento mori. Once again you have to leave it as an unsolvable riddle, as Földényi thinks. He is right in that these smoothly polished, perfect platonic bodies are simply too artificial. The monoliths of the Stone Age cultures I mentioned above represent something completely different. They are boulders erected vertically, which served an idolatrous cult at that time, possibly correlated with astronomical (sunrise etc.) events. Something 'spiritual' so to speak.

But Földényi has even more to offer. In the picture on the left you can see the field chapel, which was designed by the architect P. Zumthor in a rural area in

Switzerland. This building also has a polyhedral shape again, namely a pentagonal one. Földényi already raves about the mighty stone formation rising over twelve metres when he approaches it. It awakens in him "an  awareness of the finiteness of existence"; he speaks of how the heavy, immobile block appeared all the more dynamic when viewed over a longer period of time, although it also gave the impression of a light floating. Having entered the interior, he praises the "poetics of space" and the "catharsis of spatial experience", which all comes across as somewhat romanticising and rapturously pathetic, considering that he writes about it in over twenty pages.

Now Földényi is not a patient in a Freudian psychoanalysis, where one could easily interpret this giant tower as a phallic symbol. Therefore it is good that the author finally - as with Dürer's polyhedron - speaks of something unexplainable that surrounds all these artistic, and yet simply natural stone, blocks. Nevertheless, this field chapel reminds me of the towers of great cathedrals, which do not exactly give the impression of being symbols of faith and humility. They are probably there because of their demonstration of power, their monumental strength, power and pride. Perhaps none of this is entirely inexplicable after all.

And so I can offer an explanatory compromise and solve the riddle of all these stone colossuses without aggravating their admirers. As with Dürer and Kubrick, these stone polyhedra represent for my optics the vertical of the Ego, which - not without good reason - wants to gain recognition and confirmation. For this the Ego has to step out of the body's own reflections, out of the kaleidoscope of its imaginary, image-creating, lucidly shining, in order to become aware of its just, appropriate and valid effect to which it is entitled. Whether the stones are the best means for this, one can doubt. They show strength, power, potency, but perhaps too little meditative or even scientific truth. Admittedly, other arts, philosophies and cultural monuments are not better off.

But this book is about such a truth. Architecture, art, philosophy may be helpful for the experience of the vertical self, but in *Analytic Psychocatharsis* one can experience this vertical in oneself, one does not even need a guide, teacher or therapist. From the juxtaposition of the usual horizontal Ego and the vertical Ego, the only valid goal is the juxtaposition of the vertical Ego and the usual horizontal Ego. I could call it the diagonal Ego, in which all attributions are united. But the path leads first of all over the vertical and is above all for each Ego - as the philosopher M. Heidegger would say - the ever-its. See yourself in my paintings, says the painter, hear yourself in my words, murmurs the philosopher, but I recommend a see and hear yourself in yourself: by means of the other in you with its negativity, by means of the vertical with its negative space and by means of the combination of all of them.

It is only today that many newer psychoanalysts see the predominance of primary reflections, especially those in one's own body, i.e. the strong 'body-mirror-Ego', the psy-chic "concrete original object" (COO), which determines us from the beginning, as pre-existent anyway.[47] Anyone who has observed babies, and this is part of psychoanalytical training today, will confirm that in the first weeks the child remains self-mirroring in itself. The sucking reflex, which is still biologically determined, cannot be mistaken for the 'oral object', i.e. the lip and palate lust of the oral drive that develops.

According to Freud, the irritation of the mouth zone has the effect that the satisfaction of needs associated with food leads to a drive of its own. The child then tries to repeat this satisfaction experience by thumb sucking and other means, even though it is well-fed. Even many months later everything is still put into the mouth to satisfy this instinct, which is completely detached from the actual need. Yes, even the adult gourmet often continues this desire into the last years of his life by not making sufficient use of the erotic pleasure life, which is considered to be more mature. Of course, the same thing can happen here, namely to remain fixed in the sexual, which led Lacan to say with regard to the man: "The man is married to his phallus, he has no other woman".

[47] Ferrari, A. B., From the Eclipse of the Body to the Dawn of Thought, London: Free Association Books (2004)

The more mature enjoyment, the 'jouissance' is not achieved.

The very early body-own-mirroring is nevertheless an important soulful experience. So the child has no or only very little 'horizontal relations' and remains for some time in the 'vertical relation' to itself. Only later do the actual self-mirrorings follow, with which one reflects oneself outwardly in the other, which then also includes secondary narcissism and other vanities and cravings for recognition. In short: it is exactly that, where one as an individual starts or has to start with oneself alone anyway, before the world and society join in. One has always wanted to explain this early phase of development with questionable terms such as pre-linguistic, mentalising, performative and similar filler words.

It is also what urges people to capture the vertical in their ideas and arts, politics and cultures, even though these are all just fleeting efforts to do justice to the vertical Ego. I have already mentioned that Freud made every church tower someone dreamed of into a phallic symbol. But this psycho-analytical peculiarity refers to the phallic phase that occurs in the third to fifth years of life, which causes a certain sexual pride in both sexes equally. It is therefore a much later development than the COO phase and therefore cannot be confused with this early phase.

This earliest phase of reflection is therefore the first of the two forms of reflection, in that it is a direct reflection with one's own body, the pure Id Rays, the mirrorraying line returning to the individual.[48] In *Analytic Psychocatharsis* it also appears as a body image that can be felt, as a coenesthetically perceived body image, i.e. as the COO in the form of the body's own 'trickling through', as I will describe it later. Psychoanalyst S. Maiello describes this early form of the Id Rays as an "object of experience", in which the child experiences the warmth and the emotions of the mother as its own - possibly already in the womb - in a real visual way.

The early form of the correlating Id Speaks she calls the "sound object", because the child 'hears' the heartbeat and speech of the mother and also considers this to be its own rhythmic, echoing, sound.[49] Many primitive peoples try to use this early phase for communication by imitating the child's babbling in the first weeks of life to create a kind of sound of being together. Now these psychic 'objects' initially connect with each other in a rather chaotic way, which is typical for imaginary signifiers. This is probably the reason for the second phase, which speaks to the self-reflection in the other outside and thus to a more elaborate speech.

Here, in this second phase, it is about what everyone learns at school: self-reflection in the other outside, which is always said to be the only way to become

---

[48] I will come back to the similarity between the circle and the infinite straight line, which from a geometric point of view can explain this early phase.

[49] Maiello, S., Das Klang-Objekt (The Sound-Object), PSYCHE Nr. 2 (1999) S. 137-157

whole and authentic. Only in the other can one truly see and understand oneself (image-real) and also name oneself as an identity for oneself (word-real). For oneself one is nothing. This second reflection includes vanity, narcissism, and projective identities, while the word-real is expressed in the speech written by the Ego and other personal psychic entities. It can take superego forms, witness the truth, inner interlocutor and idealizations of the Ego (Freudian ideal Ego and Ego-ideal). It is especially this second phase of reflection that plays the main role in classical analytical psychotherapy, as I have already mentioned.

However, the first reflection, the pure body-own mirroring of the first phase, which takes place in the centre of the human being (usually in the brain) and which has been given too little consideration in research to date, is much more important and will play an important role in *Analytic Psychocatharsis*. Evolutionary biologist, C. Wills, has developed a model in this regard which explains this primary body mirroring as the beginning of being human. He spoke of the brain that has "gone through" or "ahead" with itself in the context of human development.[50]

He postulated that the enlargement, the complex development of his brain, the more complex group dynamics (which also includes the longer dependence on the mother), but above all the increasing identity problems

---

[50] Wills, C., Das vorauseilende Gehirn (The anticipating Brain), Fischer (1996) S. 20

had forced the early humans or even pre-humans to re-orient themselves, sometimes even to "go nuts", to be-havioural reversals and the loss of innate instincts. The brain had rushed too far ahead with all these demands, self-mirroring in one's own body, spontaneous 'visions', a space filled with lucidity and illumination had oc-curred, but also a state of arousal, which - once again somewhat cooled down - made the aforementioned, calmer, more constant body-Ego-mirroring (a first pleasure-Ego as Freud said) possible.

In this context, philosopher P. Sloterdijk spoke of foam-ing, of the effervescence of the brain, which has the same result.[51] Pictorial impressions have made the hu-man brain 'foam', yes, this mental growth has actually made him a human being. He now possessed an image, an - as psychoanalysts say - 'imaginary object', a very first, still little conscious Ego. S. Freud had already known this when he said: "The Ego is above all a physi-cal Ego, it is not only a surface being, but itself the pro-jection of a surface".[52] Really, a pleasure-Ego that is close to the Id Rays, close to the COO.

So it is something like a mirror-image that lingers in its own dimension for a certain moment, almost caught in its own dimension and appears as if from nowhere. This primary reflection, this archetypal image of the Ego is itself only a projection, something imaginary-real,

---

[51] Sloterdijk, P., Sphären III, Schäume (Spheres III, foams) , Suhrkamp (2004)
[52] Freud, S., GW XIII, S. 237 - 289

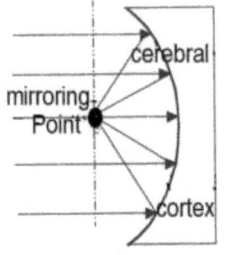

which psychoanalysts therefore call an 'imaginary object'. It is object-like and yet also pictorial and ocular. In this early reflection, which already takes place in the mother's womb and for some time after birth, there are already parts of the question whether the child corresponds to more fatherly or more motherly genes and whether it is male or female, which also contributes an aspect to today's gender and transgender discussions.

For example, the brain is scientifically understood as a hemisphere at the base of the skull, i.e. as a concave, internally reflecting layer of nerve cells that reflects rays coming from the body and other brain layers back and forth in the centre of the hemisphere (see figure right above). It is the subject and reflection point of images. Excitations and glances that radiate back and forth to this point without directly affecting the physiological visual process. It is the point of gazing-pleasure that Id Rays.[53] What is important is that it is a pure bodily, individual reflection of the individual, which appears isolated in each individual and - in the airless space, so to speak - forms the core of the first Ego in the pure surface projection.

---

[53] Psychoanalytically, it is about the part of the gaze which, due to its libidinous occupancy, is largely faded out in the process of looking and thus remains in the process of bodily reflection as one of the psychic objects mentioned by Lacan klein a.

I would like to try to explain this with the essence of the 'lucid dream', in which one is in the total mirror world of this body mirror, in virtual space, and at the same time bathes in the 'jouissance', the autochthonous enjoyment. Freud's libido seems to be "desexualized" in the autochthonous 'jouissance' as well as in this dream state, but visually, virtually, the whole thing is so perceptible in a lucid dream that one thinks it is real (real in its enjoyment), and in a certain way it is. Lacan speaks of the 'imaginary real', a purely topological figure, one of which I am depicting here (the starry sky as a Möbius

strip in the picture beside). It is a single continuous surface, which nevertheless always has two sides.

And it is in exactly this way that you get entangled whenever you travel around on one side in such a wonderful, glorious, lucid dream, and then have to wake up or fall asleep again when you arrive on the other side without realizing it. Because in the lucid dream you always end up in a place where you become completely irrational, which is also possible in a waking state when you think something paranoid. A lucid dreamer doesn't realize that a healthy desire to sleep leads him back to Morpheus, when the dream texture becomes too nonsensical.

For the pure body mirroring one has to think of the event in terms of Einstein's geometry (topology), in which the infinite straight line returns to the finite and is therefore equivalent to the circle. The circle, however, is an early form of the imaginary signifier, and not only because it is put on the finger as a ring or a chain around the neck. The discs of the moon and the sun and many other ring forms also belong to the signifiers provided by nature, which symbolise that which is closed in on itself, that which connects, i.e. the transition from the imaginary to the linguistic, the beginning of a consolidating order. I have already mentioned all this in the description of the significant lines of power.

Lacan's geometric-topological designs, which can establish a connection to the soul without any romanticism or infatuation, even if not as directly and vividly as the stone blocks, also serve this purpose. But at least, the analytical interpretations supported by topology lead from the horizontal (the patient lies on the couch) to the vertical. Lacan liked to use the image of the cross-hood, which ideally combines the horizontal and the vertical as a place of desire and claim. Conversely, in *Analytic Psychocatharsis*, here the practitioner sits in a comfortable, upright position and edits through the horizontal ideas coming from memories and current experiences until a successful, good combination of aspirations is found.

## 5. The Beauty Spot

I repeat Freud's statement, that the Ego is only the projection of a surface, only a spot in the overall picture of
man. It is something like a beauty spot, which disturbs
the fullness of human aesthetics, but which in end effect
is what makes the real attraction. A 'grain de beauté, a
birthmark, is a spot that only covers and distorts the
gaze of the Other, which would be dazzling or horrify-
ing. Because Lacan's Other, abbreviated to capital A, is
not only the unconscious partner in conversation, he can
also be a monster, because he is castrated or blocked in
his libidinous, and also in his aggressive impulses and
thus attracts negative attention. "There is a deficiency in
the Other ( $\emptyset$ therefore crossed out), and what he is
missing is a signifier. God (if one wants to understand
him as the great Other) is missing an explanation for the
evil in the world.[54] So he' s not significant enough.

The child's own desires are confronted with failures
from the very beginning on: there is always an apparent
'against', a 'no', which acts as an original repression and
thus introduces the negation of the Other into life. This
is an important story, because not only in the beginning,
but also later in life, the other will seem negative to us,
we will enter into a negative relationship with the Other.
"The negativity of the Other gives way today to the positivity of the same," writes philosopher Byung Chul-

---

[54] Lacan-entziffern.de, Die Ungerechtigkeit Gottes (The Injus-
tice of God).

Han.[55] "The violence of the same is invisible because of its positivity," he continues, "so that its proliferation becomes destructiveness, i.e. ultimately we must learn to accept such negativity, this primordial repression. A beauty spot mitigates all this.

The Freudian primal repression is like a split being of the double agent or the vertical of the stone blocks, a kind of shibboleth, a trademark of the insufficiently significant. Primordial repression is an initial displacement, it is also characterized by a fundamental psychic dichotomy or psychic fixation on an inner 'object'. Lacan again expresses himself elegiacally; for him, primordial repression is a first signifier, an unlimited and overwhelming claim of the primordial Other (I translate: the echo of everything that people have ever said, the echo of culture as such). But in addition - I believe - primal repression also results from the splitting off and denial of the COO, the primary body's own reflection.

That is why there is a first negation, a No, a fundamental lack behind this primal image-word-acting, which Lacan propagates anyway as a negative cause for all existence. Not because something is there, but because something is absolutely lacking, di the forces come into play. And that is why it is so important to build the 'vertical I' from this double of the image-word-effective in you, in order to bring it to a unity that is yourself, horizontally and vertically.

---

[55] Byung Chul-Han, 'Die Austreibung des Anderen (The Expulsion oft he Other)', Fischer (2016)

The female double agent denies this lack, because if she really wants to have clear success, she has to take an enormous risk of being exposed. She cannot hold the vertical of her Ego, which she initially built correctly from this doubling.[56] But she has only built it up from 'wrong' and 'right', as triumph and counter-triumph, as gazing and gawking, as we now know enough from smartphones. But it was already in the common photo and in Netflix series. Pictures that run away and are no longer glances that can linger, and so the double agent is unmasked because she no longer sees anything - except double pictures.

The same can be seen in the stone blocks, which hide in their imposing nature the fact that they are actually still just stone blocks that owe their lives to the faded-out driving force of the same vertical that was split off in the primal repression. "The stone weighs and shows its heaviness. But while it weighs on us, it also refuses any penetration into it. If we try to do this by smashing the rock, it will never show in its pieces an inner and open mind", writes philosopher M. Heidegger.[57] Exactly, it is a negative space that does not even show itself, but only the one behind it, which is still behind the quanta of physics itself. So Heidegger continued: "The weight of the stone is not matter, even if it is not available without

---

[56] I put the picture-acting as Cuba and the word-acting as America in this double equation.

[57] Heidegger, M., Prolegomena zur Geschichte des Zeitbe-griffs (Prolegomena on the history of the concept of time), GW Vol. 20 (1925) p. 412

matter,"[58] which demonstrates how difficult it is for philosophy to get out of the dilemma of positive and negative space, of being and not-being and all the other paradoxes.

Freud, too, would have found it easier if, instead of what he called his all-embracing 'sexual theory', had he started from the vertical Ego. A beauty spot would have remained, however, because his practice was usually too cumbersome, too word-fixed and lengthy to do justice to this vertical. And also God does not quite do justice to him, because he cannot be fobbed off with it, even if this spot is about something particularly animating. I remember a girlfriend of a dance class who wore such a mark in the middle of her cheek and whom I therefore called 'Pünktchen' (little dot), analogous to the children's novel by E. Kästner, 'Pünktchen and Anton'. Without doubt the beauty spot was an attraction.

The art historian and literary scholar Nora Abdel Rahman writes, that for Lacan, the beauty spot actually has to do with the fact that "the basis of the structure of human desire - its drama - appears in the form of a remnant, which he calls object a.[59] This object is severed or even erased and therefore never appears in the same place as desire". The beauty spot actually mitigates

---

[58] Nunold. B., Her-vor-Bringungen (Pro-po-sals), Springer Fachmedien (2003)

[59] www.nachdemfilm.de /issues /text /im-toten-winkel-der-Kamera. With this, the author describes the small a, which - as is still to be shown - can be seen at the top in the middle of the Borromean knot as Lacan's concept of desire per se.

overly erotic-aggressive desire. It beautifies it, but still remains a lifelong residue, a memorial. It remains an 'object' a and is not the 'thing'.

Freud believed that the actual, primordial, human primary desire, still strongly supported by the animalistic, also harbors forms such as incest and cannibalism, i.e. aggressively oral and aggressively phallic objects. And then it really needs more than just a corrective beauty spot, i.e. some kind of object of desire, which can only be a titillation of the palate or an addiction to money and gold. There are hundreds of such a's, which - according to Lacan - also proliferate when the capital and important L'Autre, the Other, intervenes in you and represents a certain counterweight. The Other includes internalized parents, teachers, analysts, who act as such in the unconscious as a mixture of the three areas mentioned (symbolic, imaginary, real) by showing and speaking in dreams, in the Freudian mistakes, slips of tongue or coincidences.

"As a structure," says Lacan, "this can be understood most easily at the level of the eye. There the phantasm takes hold as a visual phenomenon. According to Lacan, its structure satisfies the function of desire the most. But this desire is opposed by space, which is too positively occupied and does not establish the relationship to the body as well as its negative variant. "The function of [normal-positive] space emerges from the body, and the space appears homogeneous to the eye. Nothing in it is apparently separated. Rather, the space, always perceived as trustful, resists the cut or the division. Perception of space and body cannot therefore "mirror" the rest or the object a.

And he continues: "In the beauty spot (grain de beauté), on the other hand, the rest of it flares up. The spot interrupts the spatial homogeneity by disturbing visual unity. Human reaction to this disturbance is fear. Fear of 'always being able to grasp, to grasp every living being only as what it is in the real field of the visual signal': dummy, doll, apparition or illusion.[60] In this beauty spot the logic of the image and the logic of the word is mixed in, which points to the negative space. The effect of the image or reflection is based on an identification with the essence of the similar and bypasses the negative of the space, so to speak. In contrast, the word-acting represents an attempt to bring a statement from one to the other in a phoneme-true way, even without eye and space, and to convey the meaning in a reliable way. But just as the gaze appears as object a, as a desire to look, a curiosity, separated, unconscious, in deep space, so too the voice as object-a can only be heard as if separated from its bearer. It appears phonemic, but is not true.

The isolation of the gaze and the voice can also be well understood through hypnosis, which Freud used therapeutically at the beginning. At the beginning, the therapist holds a glittering object in front of the eyes of the test person and the person then hears only his voice in the immersion. In the after-image of the glittering, images appear which the therapist provides with clues to

---

[60] Lacan, Jacques: Die Angst (The Anxiety). Sitzung XIX (22. 5. 1963).

promote unconscious memories. But even after the return to the waking state, the memories seen in hypnosis, split off looks and the voice of the therapist remain insignificant. As with primary peoples, who rejected photographs and sound recordings they had taken as stolen glances and voices when they were tested with them, hypnosis does not lead to final therapeutic success. The gaze becomes a self glitter, the voice a faithless echo.

The early prophets could not quite unjustifiably say that they saw God: as pure brilliance, blinding light-face, whose gaze was thus severed, so that he could never be perceived as a visible face and figure. Nevertheless, this splendour is full of gaze, because the shadow, the negativity of separation, is what makes it truly a revelation. It is about "a special experience of the gazing face . . which is no longer possible today in the age of facebook. The face that exhibits itself and begs for attention is not a gazing face. There is no look within it".[61] And so today, although you are scanned by thousands of eyes in a big city, you are actually invisible. It is high time that the invisible of the gaze becomes visible and luminous again through the 'vertical self'.

It becomes visible and luminous, if you meditate long enough. For it is not unknown that the radiating point of the unconscious opens up after one has waited long enough into darkness, into nothingness. For *Analytic Psychocatharsis*, the final goal of attention, the final reality of the imaginary signifier, I will not convey the face of a god, but rather heraldry, the monstrance, the Id

---

[61] Byung-Chul Han, Im Schwarm, Matthes & Seitz (2017)

Rays of the successful combination of the two basic powers through the exercises. In other words, the combination with the Id Speaks, which is conveyed through the *pass-words*. This is no longer a process of faith, but a scientific process.

And just as the gazing face of God could not be seen, so also the voice of God could not be heard by everyone, just as it could be separated from him, it could only be proclaimed by the prophets. In the same way also do little children interrupt their monologue of falling asleep, their babbling asleep immediately when another person (another voice) comes into the room, even if the voice of this person then says nothing at all. But their echo is as if separated in the room and their gaze shimmers as if invisible in the dark. Between her monologue and the inaudible voice of the other person, however, no *pass-word* opens up for the child. Such a *pass-word* cannot be taken from the prophets either, because their mystical hearing is too much taken up by the conventional religious voices of their priests and theologians.

Look and voice, eye and ear, the image-acting and the word-acting, wander through the universe as if they were elementary forces, principles, Freudian drives. Following Lacan's two basic instincts, I call them, as already mentioned, an Id Rays (sight instinct) and an Id Speaks (speech instinct), and Lacan thus calls them signifiers, imaginary signifiers and symbolic signifiers. Now the big problem is to bring these two signifiers together, because as isolated, autonomous powers they are, according to Freud, "alloyed", i.e. somehow connected and yet completely independent, but hardly usable in most of these alloys.

This was particularly blatant when Freud spoke of the two basic forces as eros-life and aggression-death instincts, because this alloy had the form of something sado-masochistic. And yes, in a certain sense, in the light of psychoanalysis, the lofty ideals of many leaders of states turned out to be lust killings of their own or other peoples. Sadistically, women fell victim to the love of many a man, and the religious rapture of numerous masochistic believers was followed by the extermination of unbelievers. Erotic mania, extreme jealousy, greed for money and robbery, etc., all lead them to committing homicide and not to what they pretend to be: legitimate intentions and feelings. But in the end the conception of the death instinct could not be kept.

Aggression is a consequence of earliest identifications, where one sees oneself reflected in something or, as Freud said, in "a single train" of an object as if identically mirrored and unconsciously splits off other aspects of oneself,[62] from where they then return like evil demons. Thus, the actively aggressive comes mainly from the imaginary signifier, from the E flat, from the image-actor, which is difficult to tackle in classical psychoanalysis. In conventional psychoanalysis, it must be discussed and practised in hundreds of sessions, i.e. also in the difficulty to approach, which is cumbersome and arduous. It does not lead to vertical identity, which, as

---

[62] This is the third type of Freudian identification.

discussed above, is related to love of and connected to the primal Other.

I would like to add that A. Ferrari, whom I have already quoted with his COO, and who refers to this first, self-reflection of the body, understands the secondary self-internal reflection as the definitive "horizontal relation-ship", because it is reflected in the outside of social, emotional, business relationships. In contrast, he de-scribes the 'concrete original object' of the primary body-per-self reflection as the 'vertical relationship'. We are used to the outwardly directed horizont-zonal Ego, the vertical Ego we have split off, forgotten, although it would be so important. Therefore I have dedicated this book to the vertical self.

The philosopher P. Sloterdijk has already dealt with this personality structure, he only uses the terms somewhat differently than I have described them so far. So he makes fun of the body image or body scheme, which he calls the so-called 'vertical tension' and which probably has to do with the 'vertical relationship scheme' that A. Ferrari speaks of. [63]The 'above', the 'higher' and 'upper' - not only that of body sensations, but also that of reli-gions and philosophies, probably also that of his own - encourages him to make mocking remarks. Jacob's lad-der to heaven and also the 'depth psychology' are situat-ed in a vertical, for which, according to Sloterdijk, there is actually no clear justification. All attempts to give form to this vertical tension always end in acrobatics, in

---

[63] Sloterdijk, P., Du musst dein Leben ändern (You must change your Life), Suhrkamp Verlag (2009)

constantly new methods of exercise and 'anthropological techniques', which are based on an enigmatic 'summit urge', he writes.

Sloterdijk describes 'vertical tension' as the 'intellectual equivalent' of the horizontal, but this is a typically philosophical view. He cannot imagine the formation of the Ego as an important reflection of the body, as many psycho-analytical authors have described it in the meantime,[64] but sees it only in highly exaggerated thoughts. Obviously Sloterdijk's concept of vertical tension is based on precisely this 'concrete object of origin' (COO), but he does not know what to do with it. He lacks medical and above all, psychoanalytical background.

Nevertheless, the philosopher himself writes in another book about 'distancing self-enclosure', or rather the 'self-isolation effect' of hominid groups in the world, when they developed into homo sapiens and turned to their inner structure.[65] This inward-turning, this retreat into the vertical, clearly points to the primary self-reflection of the body. But the philosopher does not understand its

[64] I refer here to numerous psychoanalytical, bodymirroring theoretical authors like A. Ferrari, D. Birkstedt-Breen, T. Ogden. R. Lombardi, R. Carvalho, A. Lemma and others, who do not all explicitly speak of the 'vertical Ego'. The book 'The Body Speaks' by the latter author, however, gives a good overview of this theory of a primary self-mirroring of the body as a form of *Ego* development, which forms almost completely independently of external influences in the earliest phases of life.

[65] Sloterdijk, P., Sphären III, Suhrkamp (2004) S. 359

importance, because he recognized it in the early humans and the hominids, whom he considers inferior, and because he basically cannot think of anything concerning the 'vertical Ego'.

Because the hominids, as well as early humans, had to withdraw into themselves, they first became human beings, Sloterdijk says, so to speak, as a supplement to his thesis of "foaming of the brain", which I mentioned above. Self-enclosure, withdrawal, thus means especially into the bodily schematic vertical, because where else should one be able to self-close and withdraw? Now it would be easy to point to the old occidental mystics, but also to yoga, to Zen Buddhism and all those procedures where the vertical is also emphasized. This is exactly the function of Sushumna in yoga, for example, in which the 'main energy flow' in the middle moves vertically (see figure next to it, where I also drew a comparison with psychoanalysis).

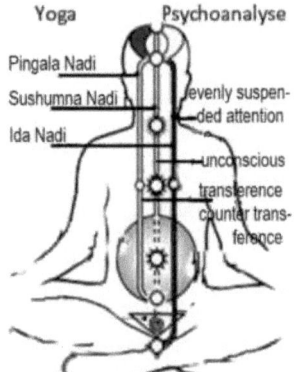

The 'vertical Ego' can be represented even better by means of a drawing that does not show the above illustration 'en face', but rather in a more suitable and factually correct lateral representation. The horizontal orientation of the gaze is marked by the black line, which runs from the front, from the eye, to the back to the centre of vision in the back of the head, where one can speak of a centre point of this line approximately in the region of the corpora geniculata (black point).

The white line is intended to indicate the vertical Ego, which has a centre in the hypothalamic area, where the 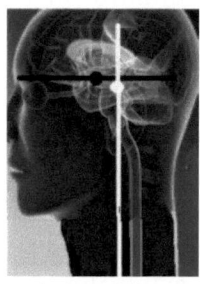 mirror-ray-point was already drawn in the figure on page 62 (here now white point). Anatomically and phys-iologi-cally, the illustration does not have to be exact, because the only important thing is that the vertical form of the Ego lies a little behind and deeper, nearer to the 'mirror-ray-point' and is not turned outwards, but remains within it-self, in the vertical of the body. This is also how one says that in meditation one has to retreat, that is, to the inside backwards, to where the basal, neuronal body im-age rests within oneself. This process is reminiscent of the statement of the founder of 'autogenic training', I. H. Schulz, that at the end of his method there should be the "vegetative changeover", psychic-nervous changeo-ver back to the primary form of the I, which is vertical.

"The subject is divided into two forms of seeing, seeing that is based on the eye, the visual system (upper trian-gle in fig. a), and seeing that is based on the gaze (lower triangle in fig. a). In a second construction step, the two triangles are superimposed on each other to show, (re-sult in fig. b next page)."[66] In humans, therefore, vision

---

[66] Nemitz, R., Das Schema von Auge und Blick (the scheme of eye and gaze) in Lacan-entziffern.de

is not regulated by the ocular-sensory apparatus alone (black line and dot in Fig. p. 81). It is also controlled by a very specific point, the light point, the Rays (white line and point in Fig. p. 81, which is located in the centre of the place formed by the concave mirror of the brain, as shown in Fig. p. 66), and which correlates ex-

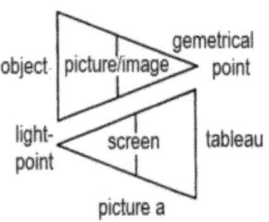

picture a

actly according to the role of the object in geometric vision with the now incomprehensible, suppressed, split-off image (tableau) of the original trauma, i.e. a pictorial emptiness. This anti-picture, in which Freud also spoke of the 'primal scene' (the frightening scene when looking into the parents' bedroom), this exciting shadow, can only be perceived through attenuation, screening (also called a screen in the middle of fig. a below), so that the glaring rays from the point of light cannot illuminate everything directly.

Both the show and its attenuation are concerned with the 'vertical Ego'. The screen acts like a light veil or foil. And so we look at the picture of a painter only from the point of view of the two triangles placed on top of each other. The painter knows how to lure something out from under the screen and give our eye something to see, the object on the canvas. That something corresponds to our desire, the desire to look, which sparkles in the point of light, rays, and yet tames our gaze at the same time, so that it does not completely flow into the canvas. For this purpose he uses the eye and - only to a varying or very limited extent - his central-perspective vision. In expressionistic and more modern painting, however, he provokes us. He increasingly leaves the perspective and exposes us to the

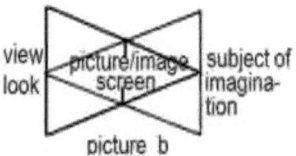

canvas/tableau. In extreme cases he approaches a horror vision or pornographic image. In the same sense, esotericists such as the anthroposophists have spoken of the point of view or ray of light as a "light or astral body". This makes it even clearer that here - as in dreams - the psychotic plays a role, not only the irrational but also the unreal.

Similarly in everyday life. In a landscape, not only the central perspective conveys to us how and what we see. Here, too, the canvas/tableau is involved, selling us domestic areas with pleasure, while others let us turn away and repress them. All this has an even stronger effect when viewing from person to person. Here, sympathy and antipathy are distributed according to the screen we have acquired, and in turn cause a wide variety of emotional and identification reactions. But ultimately, the whole essence of film and theatre that we are, cannot be grasped and nor understood solely from the field of seeing, viewing, sighting and perception. One must also draw on the field of symbolic order, language, mathematics, and the linguistically oriented signifiers (the word-acting ) that are so important in psychoanalysis and which determine the human subject just as much.

After all, I speak all the time and do not paint. I do not point, but suggest. But language alone, on the other hand, as it dominates psychoanalysis, for example, causes as much a lack, an inaccuracy, a gap, a confusion as the intersecting lines in viewing. One does not 'see' that sharply and precisely when speaking, whereas just now one could hear how much the picture, the look, the tableau, although it makes a sharp impression, but cannot tell the truth, which is why it has to hide a little in the screen/image.

The structure of screen/image, which finally stands in the middle of figure b, conveys a compromise, namely seeing through a light veil, through a barely perceptible mask, but it does not sound out of its middle in any more definite terms: "I am this or that!" It's just the Freudian "ideational representative" of the Id Rays. That of the Id Speaks must come and be explained in its own way and even more must be described how both are combined. For with thousands of images we could not establish our identity, we could not finally specify it, we need a little bit of the symbolic, of the word-acting for it.

In painting, for example, where an image is also protected by the screen of the tamed gaze, this could be a title that puts everything a little bit into its right perspective. From the point of view of light, glance, the human subject perceives itself predominantly in an autoerotic and narcissistic way, it is reflected in the glow of a 'light' that has nothing to do with physical light, but with lucidity. It is also regulated by the instinct of speaking, the Id Speaks, which intervenes in the screen with its soothing or threatening words.

At the beginning of life, the mental energies are even "present in the undifferentiated Ego-Id",[67] whereby a "primary narcissism" develops.[68] The small child, says Freud, still takes itself in a primitive way as an object of love, before it learns to love caregivers. Elsewhere he writes that this primary self-love is a counterweight against destructive tendencies (death instinct). The narcissistic self-mirror thus fends off the fear of horror. Put into the terminology of the 'vertical Ego', this would mean that it is in a lot of trouble. In other words: Freud's theory of narcissism needs to be expanded, the 'vertical Ego' needs to be built up even further.

---

[67] Freud, S., GW XVII, S. 72

[68] Freud, S., GW X, S. 154

# 6. The Vertical

The Old Testament already impressively reports about the vertical. It says there, that Yahweh went before the Israelites by day in a pillar of cloud and by night in a pillar of fire. [69]This is expressed in a wonderfully beautiful fairy-tale way, but according to today's not only psychological but probably also generally reasonable view, this is the projection of the soulful vertical to the outside. Strengthened by faith, but pushed up even further by flight and expulsion, the Israelites have been unable to keep their COO, their vertical Rays/Speaks, in any other way than to present it as projected-realized (SIR, which only became RSI in the later linguistically formulated religion).

If one follows Lacan's expansion and reformulation of the Freudian concept and sets the instinct to look and speak, to radiate and speak as primary, one can recognize in "primary narcissism" exactly this body-own-mirroring, which is also projected to the outside in early childhood. In psychoanalysis, however, this unconsciousness of a figurative, imaginary and even in adulthood still often projected nature, is only slightly processed and made conscious, unless one refers to the COO theorists, who put the emphasis on these early and very primary processes. However, one does not have to assume a death instinct, which, as I have already argued, allows everything to sink into boundless pessimism. It is also incomprehensible why the whole thing should be

---

[69] Moses 2, 13:21

called narcissism at all, self-love or self-revealing, when it is actually only about primary reflection, self-knowledge, self-disclosure. In the word 'narcissism' it gets a slightly pathological touch.

Even if Freud says here that the child takes itself as an object of love and not - as is usual in his theory - as a sexual object, it is still more about an object of joy, of glamour, of happiness - why not? Prince Narcissus falls in love with his face and does not refer to the ray-mirror point, the body-own-mirror in the subject center. Also, the word "falling in love" sounds too much like sweetly funny. If one absolutely wants to use the term love to understand this first self mirroring, one could still rather stick to the "love for oneself, that makes you happy", as psychoanalyst M. Mitscherlich titled her last book.[70] She was referring to the love of independence in her work with patients, which the American psychoanalyst G. Kohon called "detached love",[71] which the translator of this article translated somewhat strangely as 'separated love'.

This original body-own-mirroring can be seen as a love that works independently, directly, in that it is an E flat in the sense of a self-sublimation or a desire to love and to merge, a primary perception. In this most original form, seeing is being, perception is real. In order to en-

---

[70] Mitscherlich, M., Eine Liebe zu sich selbst, die glücklich macht (Love for oneself that makes you happy), S. Fischer (2013)
[71] Kohon, G., Love in a time of madness. In Green & Kohon: Love and its vicissitudes, Routledge (2005) P. 41 – 100.

dure this love gaze, the glow there, one must confront this Id Rays, the imaginary signifier, of course then the Id Speaks, the verbal signifier, as I have already emphasized several times. Both are from the beginning in the "undifferentiated Ego-Id", whereby the sound of the Speaks cannot be located as fixed as the image of the Rays. This phenomenon is also known from art: the image can be captured, fixed in memory, but not the musical tone, one must try to restore it acoustically. The field of music is far too subjective to be able to keep its elements directly in memory.

This love of self is not narcissistic or auto-erotic, it has to do with 'autochthonous enjoyment' and the 'thing' that I will discuss in detail in chapter 9. Some psychoanalysts also speak of the 'good, constant object', i.e. an inner, positively tinted firmness, and I can also compare it with the successful, good combination of Rays and Speaks. Both are often, as mentioned above, badly "alloyed", they may also have something destructive or aggressive about them, if the Ego is not yet vertically strengthened, and joy and positive certainty have not yet established themselves as the wisdom that Lacan calls that of lack.

For joy can be mixed with uncertainty or fear. The sublimation that keeps the Rays at the level of the glow and splendor, then, is in any case a way out, a beginning verticality. Freud himself had made it clear that sublimation is probably mainly moved, filled and equipped by the Eros life instinct, and so one could now add: by Id Rays, by its image-acting, by its happiness. If this is no longer sufficient in further life - and this can be the case already in the first days - the Id Speaks, the word-acting, the 'sound of nothing', signifier of lack, comes to the fore more and helps out of the jam.

With regard to this sound, I refer to an article by the science editor S. Schramm, which he entitled "The Sound of Nothing".[72] He reported about experiments of an acoustic technician in whose absolutely soundproof and also sound-absorbing room one perceives or seems to hear all possible tones and sounds after a short time. In other words: this artificially amplified extreme silence starts to thunder after a short time, as is often proverbially said. But here, too, 'sound' as such is only just significant for my project, because it has always been there from the beginning on. It represents an instinct of speaking and expression, the Speaks.

It is precisely with the 'tone', 'sound', sound that the speech-hearing system is revealed, which is not perceived in everyday life and which the psychoanalysts call the one part of the unconscious, the aforementioned Id Sounds, Id Speaks. For the psychoanalyst, these phenomena have primarily nothing to do with neurological processes in the brain. Rather, they occur in a separate area of primary enjoyment of bodily, but psychologically structured processes, which is described as unconscious. But no matter how one wants to name this exactly, the "sound of nothingness" already points out the

---

[72] Schramm, S., Der Klang des Nichts (The Sound of Nothing), South German Newspaper from 7. 11. 2016, P. R7

special depth and exclusivity of this 'sounding' or 'wording'. Here something or someone sounds, here Id Speaks, even if it is only a 'sound'. It is not about a mystical happening, but about the power of the 'drive' that urges you to express yourself, because someone is there, because you are not alone when you come into the world. A stronger hold in the vertical already is offered at the beginning.

In Freud's concept, the primary action of the two basic drives is later complicated in a pronounced way by external love objects (which include other people). In this way, love objects are abandoned and returned to identifications, which is then called secondary narcissism. Everybody knows this narcissism, when self-love is trickily connected with object-love and the identities are presented as positive-valuable. But Freud did not elaborate further on how the early body's own reflection, radiance, and the 'sound of nothing', primary speech, can always be sufficiently included in the therapeutic process. Thus, classical psychoanalysis deals only with secondary narcissism and the often insufficient "free associations", both of which are already integrated in object relationships.

With the concept of primary narcissism, conventional psychoanalysis has so far stayed out of the problem. As the authors J. Laplanche and J.-B. Pontalis write in their Handbook of Psychoanalysis, opinions on this subject fluctuate between an 'autoerotic' state and a 'primary object love', which is already built up intrauterine to the mother.[73]  But Lacan is right, it is the state of a primary deficiency, of an absence, a minus One at the beginning of human existence. However, each individual can compensate for this deficiency by reviving the verticals within himself and therefore continue to theorize further.

In *Analytic Psychocatharsis*, in the first exercise, the proximity of the Rays is specifically sought out in the form of the subject point and verticality, whereby the libidinous looking comes into consciousness, but it is kept in check by the repetition of the *formula-words* and other basic conditions (see description in the appendix) and is purely supplied to intensified self-sublimation. Freud did not want to look into the glowing eyes of the sphinx, as psychoanalyst J. Le Soldat remarked. **She declared Freud's dream of 'Irma's injection', which Freud called the dream that revealed the essence of dream to him, as to have been misinterpreted by Freud himself.[74]

Freud was to have excessively described only the libidinous aspects of his dream, not mentioning the aggressive ones. This is how Le Soldat interprets the sentence: "Irma, whom I immediately take aside to ... " in this dream, so important for psychoanalysis, that Freud wanted to get rid (in German: beseitigen) of someone

---

[73] Laplanche, J., Pontalis, J.-B., Vokabular der Psychoanalyse, Suhrkamp (1973)

[74] Le Soldat, J., Eine Theorie menschlichen Unglücks (A Theory of Human Disaster), Fischer (1994)

here, namely his already expected sixth child. But Freud is also said to have wanted to eliminate a homosexual relationship with a colleague who appears in the dream, following Le Soldat's conclusions. One must admit that Le Soldat plausibly substantiates these interpretations with numerous examples, even if they do not contradict Freud's views of the dream as a wish that is presented as fulfilled. It may well be that, in the final analysis, other wishes than Freud admits, are hidden in this dream.

Ultimately, according to Le Soldat, the sphinx is the central point in the Oedipus Saga, namely after the killing of the father and before the sexual relationship with the mother. The sphinx conveys in fairy-tale form the basic problem of martial sexuality, in which men not only kill their fathers, but also rob them of their sex, and offer large phalli to the mothers and women, which the latter want to be penetrated by. But does not all this fall short? One remains stuck in the wildest, sexist fantasies and does not come to self-rescue, expressed from the unconscious itself, to a conscious, picture-word-real ( Rays / Speaks related ) identity. Despite this, verticality is inherent in Le Soldat's theories.

Freud is, so to speak, beaten by her with his own weapons, his "primary narcissism" proves to be autosexist, and the cultural and social discourse is still exuberantly psychoanalytically normative. In short: as writer Anna M. Ortese put it a long time ago with regard to Naples: "In this dark trench, only the fire of the sexual shone under the black sky of the supernatural".[75] There is nothing between the two extremes. But an Ego-vertical is there, albeit badly alloyed, but it can be used.

In addition to the body's own mirroring of itself as the real Id Rays, also the Id Speaks as the real word of identity or *pass-word* could be brought together in a successful, authentic and real way, if one would only apply the node-key point to oneself, as it is possible in *Analytic Psychocatharsis*. In the second exercise of *Analytic Psychocatharsis*, attention is therefore paid to the 'tone', ring, 'sound', which can condense into the Id Speaks. Then the 'sound of nothing' becomes the voice of the Other, which is also the voice of nobody, because the Other has no name. Even if Lacan thus insists on the "father name" as the target point in the unconscious-verbal signifier, he does not want us to listen to a concrete person, even to a god, or even to the isolated Freud himself as the father of psychoanalysis.

Listening to the *pass-word* is the alternative and supplementation of the vertical Ego. The essence of the *pass-word* can best be explained with a further example. It came to me some time ago while practicing this second exercise of *Analytic Psychocatharsis*: "He is at the top of the o n e s," it said. At the top of the o n e s? Perhaps it means something narcissistic or egotistical, and I immediately applied the phrase thus heard to myself, adding for my own protection that it is far from being as ideal as the phrase that the deaf woman sent to Jesus:

---

[75] Ortese, A., M., Il mare non bagna Napoli, Gli Adolphi-Verlag (1953)

"This is my beloved son, with whom I am well pleased. This divine dove-*pass-word*, however, sounded almost too good, too pathetically good, but what about mine?

Certainly, I was at the top of this phrase, but only at the top of the o n e s, the neutrals, impersonals and colourless o n e or o n e s. I can't gloss over anything, the o n e's are perhaps my readers, most of whom I don't know. But maybe that's just as well, I love my o n e s, and maybe that's just because they don't get too close to me and still allow me to be upfront? There is something alternating between the o n e s and the top.

"One relieves the respective existence in its everyday life. . . The One, with whom the question of the Who of everyday existence is answered, is the Nobody, to whom all existence in being among each other has ever been at the mercy of. . . The Who is the Neutrum... . Everyone is the Other and no one is himself."[76] I could enthusiastically quote from chapter III, 27 of Heidegger's book, which revolves endlessly around this denial of one's own life through the conformity of the o n e s. To pass only through the fear and apparent death of the self, enables one's own being and revolt with the overcoming of too much o n e s. For the o n e's are not all that bad, for "actual selfhood is not based on a state of exception of the subject detached from one, but is an existential modification of the o n e s as an essential existential," Heidegger writes in conclusion: One only has

---

[76] Heidegger, M., Sein und Zeit (Being and Time), Niemeyer Verlag (1963) S. 126-129

to apply the o n e correctly, then one can also stand out front, I ultimately interpreted my *pass-word*.

But I also heard the negativity, mockery, the smugness of this *pass-word* coming out of him. So I have to be content to be at the head of a certain not very personal, but existentially valuable crowd. I have to realize that I cannot have a close, meaningful and self-supporting relationship with everyone. The top is not particularly high, is perhaps only a small skewer that stings me - anti-narcissistically, so to speak. So in reality the saying is actually: "He is o n e without a spike", and it is the o n e s who, as independent, should build up the important relationships more to themselves and to others with the help of a procedure that also another could have invented. But my o n e s invented it.

Ever since Lacan's psychosemiotics, something like this was in the air to develop a method which can be used like the 'linguistic crystal' (a term of Lacan for the unconscious) of the formula- and *pass-words*. But there is one thing - I think I am right in thinking so - that the *pass-word* example conveys, namely how curious, how 'the other way round', how strangely imaginative the unconscious expresses itself from its deepest core. No writer would ever come up with such sentences, yet the whole thing sounds like the Delphic Oracle, which I always had to interpret in order to grasp its final truth. So I will still have to work on it.

The horizontal Ego, the "horizontal relationships" of everyday encounters and social-psychological conditions, which are now strongly dominated by the voice of the Other in and around oneself, must therefore be contrasted with the "vertical Ego" of the vertical body-self-mirroring, in that it can be erected by the Rays and held in the vertical by Speaks. Bringing the two together, successfully, real combined, they would produce the true and mature personalities that are so desperately needed. In the following, I will describe the subject matter even further to make it more conclusive. From its practical side, *Analytic Psychocatharsis* is quite simple to perform, but the framework to be understood intellectually is also important.

## 7. Quantum Psychology

It has always been a fascinating and interesting task to be able to define the connection between spirit and matter, soul and brain, conscious and unconscious psyche and other similar things more precisely. But so far it has not been possible to describe this connection plausibly or even scientifically in a direct form, and - I say it in advance - it will not be described in this book, either. Esoteric, mythical, philosophical, mystical and comparable works have claimed a result of this connection, but they have not found a scientific basis even approximately. Even physicists have not managed to create the predicted world formula of the so-called 'all-encompassing theory'. They are still fumbling around between the quantum mechanics of N. Bohr and W. Heisenberg and Einstein's theory of relativity, and now claim to have come up with at least one approach in the most daring theories (supersymmetry, string theory) that could unite the forces of the very small and the very large.

In doing so, they are narrowing their own minds to the premises that natural science imposes on them. Although they can actually prove something, they always remain one step behind the human subject. They cling to the so-called objective, but always have to disassemble, reduce, enlarge and reify the object in other ways in order to keep themselves out of the game as human subjects. They consider the subject to be unpredictable and thus fortify themselves from their own unconscious thoughts. In other words, they keep their gaze lowered and focused on the ground of material facts, even when they look into the universe with ever newer and more technically sophisticated equipment. They do not explain their role as investigators, they do not give up their fear, when nowadays we know that at the most objective moment the investigator himself is involved in subatomic realms. So they are also slaves to the technology they claim to be founding.

But even humanistic scientists do not function better here and are just as much, if in a different way, one step behind. The philosophers, for example, have to think up this connection (spirit / matter etc.) and cannot really prove anything they say. They do justice to the subject, but not to the factual. Philosophy and theology and everything that has been tried to be established on the basis of conscious concepts, finally returns to the conscious starting point via new concepts, symbols, signs, systems etc. They take a unit that is significant from the beginning (e.g. the idea or the being) and then give it back as newly defined and found (in other words: they pull the canine out of the hat that they put in there before).

Now, between these two major fields (natural sciences and humanities), there are numerous people who often even have an academic title, but fill the gap with self-made theories. One of the first physicists to argue in questionable ways on how spirit and matter are connected, was Capra, with his 'Tao of Physics', in which he compared the question of space-time with the notion of emptiness in Zen Buddhism. He also wondered whether quark symmetry (i.e. the order of the smallest elementary particles) was not a new koan, i.e. structured like a

Zen Buddhist riddle word.[77] So Capra is a physicist and feels that physics only has a chance, if it includes the human subject in its statements, in the participant's perspective! The philosopher Hastedt had already previously postulated that "the mind in the participant's perspective as the subject of cognition is methodologically superior to mind and body as objects of cognition in the observer's perspective".[78]

And in this sense Capra observed a fascinating analogy between mind and matter. But the Koan - and so one must punish people with their own language - lies beyond any concept of science! It is a wonderful tool of the old Taoist psychotherapy and leadership, but it cannot be included in our western scientific culture. Sometimes it even becomes a bizarre and aggressive farce as for example in 'quantum psychology' of A. Wilson, an American 'multitasking' esotericist. This self-proclaimed scientist had a large following, wrote many books and was nothing but a quantum and network fanatic.

He rightly relied on indeterminacy, on the uncertainty relation of the above mentioned quantum mechanics and then he could see that indeterminacy is common in all areas of life. Of course, this is not necessarily something new, but the problems are obvious. He used only bold analogies and the principle of similarity. Thus he saw similar structures in the networked brain and in the universe as given and processes as equally effective, so that

---

[77] Capra, F., Das Tao der Physik, Scherz Verlag (1987) S. 246

[78] Hastedt, H., Das Leib-Seele-Problem (The Body-Soul-Problem), Suhrkamp (1989) 291

one could influence gifts in the environment via the common element of psychic, mental, neuronal-spiritual. But how is this to work in the end, when similarities are not equalities as demanded by mathematics, and analogies are not real logics.

The feminist and physicist Barad goes even further. In her statements on the phenomenon of 'entanglement' (two photons are entangled with each other by quantum action, although they themselves are far apart, remote action) she also relies on the theory of complementarity of the physicist N. Bohr and also on the deconstructivism of the philosopher J. Derrida.[79] Barad further confirms the view of the uncertainty relation by saying that the measuring instrument and the object to be measured are separate, but on the other hand they are completely 'entangled' and interwoven. The human observation apparatus itself interacts with the observed. How do you want to measure exactly? But not only do the objects and the measuring instruments behave in a complementary way, the latter also behave among each other. This leads to a different and extreme view of 'remote effects', but it can only explain physics with philosophy and not define it by itself.

In doing so, she leaves a more strict mathematical-physical view. For whatever else may be going on between measuring instrument and object, since it is a uniform process to which both are related, it is no longer so

---

[79] Barad, K., Verschränkungen (entanglements), Merve (2015)

clear and precise when it comes to measuring instruments. Do the measurements then double or cancel each other out? From a mathematical-physical point of view, a unit (entity) that is effective in physics cannot be at two points at the same time, otherwise it takes on an irrational form that is subject-related. That is why the physicist M. Esfeld thinks, that in all these cases of 'remote action', "a precise definition of 'measurement' is not given at all.

That is also not possible. Because physically there is no difference between a measurement process and any interaction. Furthermore, measuring devices are not natural objects that occur in nature independently of our interests, such as electrons, oxygen atoms, DNA sequences. . . Rather, arbitrary things can be used as measuring devices by experimenters according to their intentions".

And further: "If one accepts definitive numerical values for properties of macroscopic objects . . . and if one accepts quantum mechanics as a complete description of microphysical reality, then one has to incorporate the possibility of transition to well-defined numerical values into the dynamics used for the time evolution of quantum systems".[80] In other words: In quantum mechanical entanglement, as already mentioned above, the measuring instruments are ultimately quantum mechanically constructed and interactions can no longer be measured. This is already evident today in the attempt to construct

---

[80] Esfeld, M., Das Wesen der Natur (The Essence of Nature), Spektrum der Wissenschaft, 6/11, S. 57

the first quantum computers. They have to be cooled down almost to absolute zero, must not be exposed to minimal vibrations and must be made only of certain metals. Their sensitivity to error is therefore immense, and so these computers will only be available with a certain degree of limitations with which conventional computers will probably still be able to compete.

Nevertheless, I will try to describe one of these fascinating analogies, which I criticized above as being too little scientific, in more detail. It's about physical string theory and the knot chains of Lacan. The former is based on the assumption that there are wafer-thin 'vibrating strings' that traverse the universe in short or even incredibly long form and can represent, mediate and justify both the elementary particles and the gravitational waves. String theory is an achievement of modern physics, which has almost succeeded in uniting the above-mentioned two areas of Einstein's theory of relativity (simplified: the theory of the very large, i.e. stars and gravity) and quantum mechanics (theory of the very small, i.e. elementary particles) founded by N. Bohr. For almost a century one had to live with the fact that each of these two physical concepts were correct and conclusive in themselves, but it seemed impossible to combine them. Although they belong to the same natural science and mathematics and although they dealt with the same substances of the universe, they could not be married or renounced (if I may say so lasciviously).

String theory has now more or less succeeded in clarifying the problem of so-called dark matter and dark energy. Dark matter and dark energy have long been known as mysterious monsters in the universe, because they take up several times the amount of visible matter and measurable energy. Dark matter can be proved, for example, by the fact that it shows clear gravitational effects. So it must really exist, but one cannot see it, because it does not emit light and radiation. It is similar with dark energy, because it is needed to explain the expansion of the universe. What is it that drives the stars apart, where all their forces only affect each other and are attracted to each other?

The help of string theory in this respect is that it starts from a multiverse composed of two, three or more universes, and one of these sub-universes (say, for example, ours) interacts with another such sub-universe or parallel universe in a very specific minimal form. This interaction is primarily carried by the gravitational waves or gravitational force particles (also called gravitons). But how, has up to now remained a mystery. So strings are like ultra-thin threads, taut strings, which can oscillate and thus, on the one hand, express the nature of elementary particles. In their closed form, on the other hand, in which they thus close round, they have to do with gravity and establish the connection to the parallel universe. This connection, this connecting passage or tunneling through, which was also called "wormhole" because of its small size, is not provable and perhaps never will be, but if one can very plausibly conclude that it is a wormhole, it has a great significance.

Through this tunneling connection, gravity, the effect of large masses and energies that remain dark, comes into our universe. In short: our existence, as it happens here on earth, is controlled to a greater extent by a world to which there is no access. This other world of closed strings, which itself also houses masses and energies, seems like the beyond, which religions have called the 'sky' dominating us for thousands of years. The main forces lie over there on the other side, always unknown, and only through the narrow tunnel of a revelation is there contact to it. On the other hand, the elementary particles that plague us with their quantum mechanics are buzzing around in the more worldly world.

Or, explained differently: recently, physicists found within metal bodies, e.g. at their border regions, that electron flux is stronger, faster, resp. with less resistance, than inside the metal piece. This distribution of electron flow, described as the quantum Hall effect, is similar to topological figures, such as the torus (tubular tire), whose vectors (see arrows 1 and 2 in the illustration below) do not circle around a defined center point. Is it again human observation apparatuses, is it human / machinery interactions, that lead to this? M. König, also a physicist, has developed curious ideas on this.

In his book, he is not only concerned with the ideas of entanglement, but also with the creation of an original language, which he wants to bring into harmony with physics.[81] He calls this harmony the 'original word'.

---

[81] König, M., Das Urwort (The original Word) , Scorpio (2010)

Everything seems extremely speculative and finally seduces the author to assert communication (even such of a highly philosophical nature?) between the living and the dead by means of "bundled essence electrons", if they only have enough "electromagnetic energy density". "Electrons are elementary units of consciousness", he writes, "the soul is a plasma state, a gas". But König becomes quite bold by applying his theory in practice.

It looks like this: you sit down under a large "gold torus" (see figure below). This topological structure reminds of the orgone accumulator of W. Reich, a student of S. Freud, which brings us back to psychoanalysis.

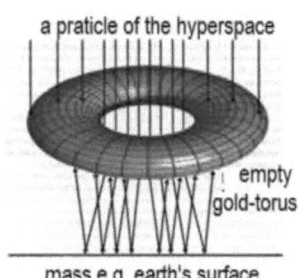

a praticle of the hyperspace

empty gold-torus

mass e.g. earth's surface

Reich had used a cube made of different conducting and non-conducting materials to achieve exactly these transformation, transdimensional effects as described by König. Einstein tested this device, but could not explain its effects with usual physical effects. He considered it to be unreal. In addition, the subject, the speaking side was missing in this discussion.

While König tries to include them (he is concerned with the original word mentioned in the title), his construction of this original word from magic letter plates falls far

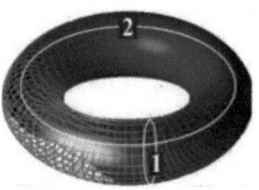

short of the Lacanian signifiers. On the other hand, his metal torus sounds like the quantum Hall effect of official physics, for which was awarded the Nobel Prize. But König was not yet familiar with this new research and their results, otherwise he might have found it easier to derive his gold torus from them and draw far-reaching conclusions for the relationship to the brain or - even better - to the unconscious. For therein lies the precarious fascination of a universal key that should work in all situations.

And here I can now make the leap to Lacan's psycho-analysis. There is also a dark, difficult to see connection, which would very aptly deserve the name "worm-hole". It is the connection between the Ego and its conscious feelings and thoughts and the unconscious, which has remained mysterious until today, through very similar tunnels, which Lacan calls "défilés logiques", logical narrowings. The unconscious is not the subconscious, as is often reported. The unconscious is unconscious in a quite blatant way, it works like a parallel universe within ourselves and like the physical parallel universe it can only be proved indirectly. In dreams, promises, mistakes and spontaneous, thoughtless associations of the patient in the psychoanalytical session, this deep-soul parallel universe sometimes comes out in its twisted logic. More and more it shows its incredibly strong and versatile effect on the conscious mind.

Just as in astrophysics dark matter takes up more space and time than visible matter, so the unconscious has probably much more validity and effect than our Ego including its attributes. And indeed, the whole thing seems to happen as if through a "wormhole", a 'défilé', a bottleneck, whereby one has the feeling that this aspect alone has two basic functions, namely that of 'similarity', which Lacan also calls a first dialectical category[82] and which I would speak of as an insufficient, even if fascinating category. It is close to the ray, to the image-creator, to the imaginary signifiant edge, which leads to something like the correspondence of network structures in the brain and the universe, as I quoted A. Wilson.

The second basic function is that of Otherness, in that it represents the counter-universe or even the multi-universe, where the laws of physics supposedly no longer have to apply. Lacan also speaks here of the "défilés signifiantes", the logical narrownesses, the imaginary/symbolic tunnels through which unconscious images and meanings torture themselves in order to arrive at appearance and logical consciousness. Here, too, the word 'engulfment', 'défilé', seems to say it all. Here, something is like being put through a meat grinder, and isn't it the grinder itself that carries the main meaning within itself?

Yes, because with Lacan you can find threads, strings (rond des ficelles), which can be open or closed (e.g. ring-shaped) and loop through the mentioned tunnels. In closed form, they look like a Borromean knot in which three (sometimes more) of these threads are looped around each other in such a way that it is a closed structure (see next chapter). But if you open only one of

---

[82] Lacan, J., Seminar II, Walter, 1980, S. 180

these loops, they are all loose and free, just like the freely swinging strings. There are several reasons why a loop can open - more about that later. At the moment I am only talking about this because these thread formations (rond des ficelles) have such a pronounced similarity with the strings.

Again it is about similarity, about strong analogy, which scientist D. Hofstadter called a naive, trivial analogy, because he thought that such analogies have a real scientific proof character. But as mentioned above, this is not quite true. Again and again something subjective comes into play, but is not explained exactly. The basic function of 'similarity' is close to the Rays, to the image-acting, to the imaginary signifier. In Hofstadter's work, however, it is supplemented by the second, the symbolic order (verbal signifier, Speaks). In psychoanalysis, the interlocking of the two categories can now be brought from analogy (via the catalogue of various technical terms) to dialogue. Such a thing can rather be called science.

But as perfect as the psychoanalytical theory formation is revealed here, the disadvantage for my project of bringing spirit and matter together is that no dialogue can be conducted with the parallel universe. The analogies are correct and the catalogue of terms (e.g. the agreement regarding the tunneling) can also be used in this way, but there is no symbolic order in the parallel universe. Or is there? I would like to suggest, how one could get closer to the mind-matter-problem in a more precise way.

In addition, again briefly to Lacan. Besides the symbolic (word-acting) and imaginary (image-acting), he introduces the real as third (e.g. third loop in the Borromean knot). But the real is not external reality. It is not factual, but active. Freud spoke of psychic reality, but this is too contradictory) Because the psychic unconscious is just active, except for picture- and word-acting, I would have to call it the active-effective or better the real-acting. Now, Lacan connects this real-working person with mathematics, which, although 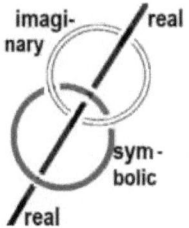 there is a certain reality, which can also be behind the outer reality, but in general is so abstract, so unrealistic, a real paradox.

That is why I propose a way that is also used by mathematics, but which is above all based on an improved and special treatment of the symbolic and imaginary and thus approaches the real-acting. In addition again an illustration of the Borromean knot, whereby one of the loops, namely that of the real, is drawn as an 'infinite' straight line (in the next chapter I will show in how far the circular loop and the 'infinite' straight line are completely equivalent, i.e. can be drawn one way or the other). I don't have to say anything else about the imaginary, the pictorial is never unambiguous, it has no definite order of its own, it always presents itself as a flood of images, which can lead to hallucinations in the unconscious. The same is true in the universe, where we find the flood of images of galaxies, nebulae, stars, planets, comets, etc. An order can only be brought there, if one takes the symbolic into account, as it is also the case in the unconscious and in the practice of psychoanalysis.

But as already mentioned, the universe with its parallel form does not speak, there is no symbolic order. Rather, astrophysicists fall back on natural science and thus tinker with string theory and supersymmetry, for example. Now, however, astrophysicist M. Pössel describes something that proves that interesting sounds occur in the universe, just as in the psychoanalytical consulting room. In the case of neutron stars (closed or semi-closed strings), he was able to determine a sound phenomenon that comes close to Morse code and could thus possibly actually yield something linguistic.

"Small disturbances of space-time geometry - small deviations from the geometry of absolutely empty space-time can propagate as waves.[83] We know a similar way of propagation from sound waves: a small area of air is slightly denser and therefore has a higher pressure than its surroundings, so it expands a little, which in turn leads to higher density, pressure and slight expansion in the neighbourhood, and in this way the excess density is propagated further and further. In Einstein's case, it is a small space-time distortion that leads to a further space-time distortion in the neighbourhood, so that the disturbance ultimately propagates through the whole of

---

[83] The sections quoted here and in the following are from the astrophysicist Markus Pössel "The wave nature of gravitational waves" in: Einstein Online Volume 3 (2007), p. 1106

space, at the speed of light. These propagating perturbations are the gravitational waves."

"In the simplest case of such a wave, the distortion can be caused as follows (figure below). Assuming we are once again in space, far away from all gravitational sources. On the floor of our spaceship cabin we place the following mandala image (above) made of grains of sand of different colours. A simple gravitational wave running through this mandala distorts the distances between the sand particles as shown in the animated image (direction of arrow). In the case shown, the wave is running from behind the pictures towards the viewer, crossing the mandala. The interplay of lengthening and shortening of the distances - stretching in one direction, simultaneous compression in the other - and the fact that the distortions take place in a plane perpendicular to the direction of propagation are general characteristics of gravitational waves".

It is about "gravitational waves emitted [in this way] by

astronomical objects, which in some ways resemble more an orchestral sound than an image. What we get from a pair of neutron stars orbiting each other is not an unrelated mixture of many small contributions from which the detailed structure of the formation area can be reconstructed, but a harmonic overall wave that contains information about its large-scale formation process. In fact, the analogy goes even further, because the frequencies of some gravitational waves are in the same frequency range as those of a completely different type of wave - namely the sound waves that we can hear with our ears".

"These gravitational wave signals can therefore be 'translated' into audible sounds. . . if one transfers the frequency of the gravitational wave signal and its temporal development to sound, one can make certain cosmic processes audible. By the radiation of gravitational waves such a double star loses energy and the density distribution in the center of a supernova could then become directly 'audible'. Translated into audible tones, this corresponds to a kind of 'chirping' - a tone that begins quietly and deeply and then becomes higher and higher and louder. For astrophysicists, direct evidence of such 'chirping' is highly interesting - the course of the 'chirping' contains information about the strength of the gravitational waves emitted".

So there are indeed sounds and rhythms that only need to be translated into verbal language to have graviton or string psychology verified. There is no doubt that the gravitational waves, which are closed strings, have a strong relationship to 'Id Sounds', Id Speaks. Here we have before us the signifiers that nature provides as the first authoritative thing. But one must not believe that one signifier can directly answer another signifier, as mysticism and esotericism claims or as it tells of the good life of its trees. There lies the gross error of all pseudo-science as it was also common in antiquity and as I have just criticized above in terms of quantum and quark psychology. The chirping of gravitational waves is after all a Speaks, but the problem lies again in the question, how alloyed is this with the Rays? Is it possible to put together something solid for a psychoanalytical string theory from all the talk I have quoted here? The chirping does not make a logical statement.

No, you can't hear logic. But could it possibly involve *Analytic Psychocatharsis*? Yes, it works in a way that can definitely be described, which I will pursue in the following. For, as in psychoanalysis, neither a natural science nor a humanistic science is used in *Analytic Psychocatharsis*. However, psychoanalysis has been repeatedly denied a scientific standard until today. Now Lacan has elevated it to the rank of a "logical practice" or a conjectural science (presumption science), as it is used a lot in mathematics.[84] Nikolaus von Cues already wrote in his work 'De Conjectura' (about conjecture) that one well-founded step after the other leads to such a condensation and precision of the statements that the last step - which then has to be taken by everyone - is of itself the truth, the result of the scientific search.

So the real is mathematical after all, where assumptions are proven, but just as the unconscious is sought out in *Analytic Psychocatharsis*, it can keep up with this math-

---

[84] As is well known, there is talk of Fermat's or Poincar's conjecture, which must then be proved by purely mathematical or geometrical methods, which has already been successful for the two examples mentioned.

ematics. In my books 'The Mathematics of Eros' and 'Conjectural Thinking' I have written about this in detail. But here, at this point, I don't have to repeat everything, because I let each individual do the very last step in the further procedure - whether it is called scientific, psychocathartic analytical, conjectural-mathematical or otherwise "logically practical" - by himself. For this purpose I have quoted Hastedt's comment on the body-mind problem.

As in any meditation, one first sits facing nothingness, the dark, allegorically speaking: the parallel universe. Again, at the beginning, it is about the flood of the imaginary, which, however, can be kept well in check by the symbolism of the *formula-words*. But where is the real? In *Analytic Psychocatharsis*, the real lies in the method in which the two basic signifiers are combined, alloyed, namely by the most compact, most concrete, most "logically practical" form, which also appears possible from a mathematical point of view. For here, there is a mathematical solution in the form of *pass-words*, which each individual - and thus following Hastedt's axiom exactly - can only gain for himself.

After all, I believe that my argumentation goes far beyond that which the poet and scholar J. Peter Hebel put forward over two hundred years ago. He too wanted to relate the "body of this world" to the "body of the future", exactly as I have tried to do here, namely matter and spirit. Regarding his leaps of thought between the two categories, Ph. Theisohn writes in a commentary on the newly published complete works of Hebel: "Whether it deals with basic theological questions or with the doctrine of perspective, whether it is Moses Mendel-sohn's lectures or entomological findings . : Lebel's writing is always supported by the conviction that all this is held together by one truth. And that it is not nec-essary at all to pronounce this connection, but that it "arises as if of its own accord from the transformation of the world into words - no matter what their origin may be".[85]

The 'as if by its own accord' reminds of the interpreta-tion in case of long preserved and strengthened trans-mission, that is: unconsciously spontaneously out of each individual, and the one truth is about nothing else but the truth found scientifically, "logically practically". It is always about the same thing, to have realized the unity of body and soul, but one cannot really say this. Only each individual can experience it for himself. How he then passes it on, after the individual has experienced it and wants to put it into practice, is another question that I will discuss in the following. Because I do not want to found a new New Age movement, a scientific club, an established community of *Analytic Psychoca-tharsis* practitioners. Such a thing would only really weaken the found results again.

For it is clear that the real is at stake, if one can hear the chirping and the speech of the neutron stars also from the parallel universe and see the radiance of all the pic-

---

[85] Theisohn, Ph., Was das Auge niemals sah (What the eye has never seen), FAZ vom 7. 12. 2019, S. 12

torial glances and gaze-images. I refer again to the 'objects' of the word-working ('sound', chirping, Id Speaks as a voice) and of the image-acting (Id Rays as gaze, glow, 'endogenous image patterns' etc.).[86] I am thinking again of the negative space of the art theoretician L. F. Földényi, which opens up as a carrier of the real, in which not necessarily a god or a ghost appears, but an 'other way round' of one's own images and memories, a lucidity of one's own vertical, the 'trickling' of the body image from top to bottom, which always conveys the feeling that one is happy, inspired and not alone.[87]

Because there is not only negative space, there is also a negative time. This is not time travel backwards, as esoterics like to imagine, but a deeper penetration at the moment when the echo, the "echoes of the body",[88] which mix with those of the universe, can be heard as *pass-words*. The *pass-words* create identity for the practitioner, an identity that psychoanalysts call the "good, constant object". It is the moment to which Goethe said, " linger a moment, you are so beautiful," because only

---

[86] Eichmeier, J., Höfer, O., Endogene Bildmuster (Endogenous image patterns), U&S – Verlag (1974)

[87] One of my female patients heard a voice saying the latter to her after the death of both parents.

[88] It is all the verbal, symbolic things that have accumulated like 'echoes in the body' and of which Lacan says (Seminars XXIII, Translation Lacan Archive, p. 10): "The philosophers . . do not know that the drives are the echoes in the body. . Because the body has some openings, the most important of which, because it cannot be closed, is the ear, what I have called the voice as responding in the body".

in the moment of elevation can the truth, even the negative, be told. So this truth does not reverse time, but deepens it.

The whole thing also has something to do with mathematics and can therefore be presented even better. Despite the progress in mathematics through set theory, it is still not clear how to empirically arrive at the first integers. For the set as such is not equal to a round whole, a 'one' (Greek 'hen' and not monos). Lacan therefore suggests the following: not a one is at the beginning of arithmetic, but a "one is missing", i.e. the empty set. It only becomes a set when it has an element.

The 'one missing', the -1, is at the beginning because the whole of psychoanalysis is based on it. A fundamental lack exists not only in every suffering, but also in every speaking of it. The great ancient sceptic Pyrrhon already expressed this in this way. He accepted all phenomena, that is, what I have just called the Rays, but not that anything can be said about them, that is, that they speak. But because of this he lived very dangerously, because there were no possessions for him, and so he always walked through all the properties and gardens, so that his friends had to protect him constantly from threatening owners and biting dogs. It would have been better if he had practiced *Analytic Psychocatharsis*.

## 8. Infinite straight Line and Circle

I therefore return to my suggestion to use a different approach to science as such, where the principles of similarity and analogy are no longer used, but only that of equality or identity, as established in mathematics and its equal sign. In doing so, I start out from the mathematically, geometrically, topologically simplest form possible, namely from the 'infinite' straight line and circle mentioned above, which are, despite their apparent dissimilarity, completely equivalent, that is, they are identical. This fact can already be seen from the fact that even on the mini-sphere, which represents our Earth in relation to other planets or stars, one does not perceive the circular curvature, but always has the impression of walking on an endless straight line. How much clearer this becomes when one imagines the largest possible circle that can exist, the line of which could not be distinguished from the so-called 'infinite' straight line by the best means.

Moreover, the paradoxes and problems of infinity have long been known in mathematics. One has tried to solve it by putting together groups of numbers, e.g. the group of prime numbers, the Galois groups and others, which prevents one from constantly having to think about the concept of infinity, which is unreal. Even a ray of light is not infinitely straight; we know that starlight is bent by the gravity of other stars. Therefore, there is no difference between the circle and the 'infinite' straight line. The two mathematical-topological structures overlap, cross and knot each other as desired. Especially with the nodes, many different kinds can be represented, which are important for my further argumentation.

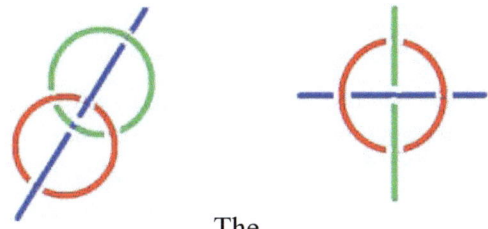

The                    fig-
ure above shows the Borromean node in various combinations of circle and 'infinite' straight line (left with two circles and an 'infinite' straight line, right with one circle and two 'infinite' straight lines, all equivalent to each other). One could also lay three 'infinite' straight lines overlapping and crossing each other, but they cannot be drawn (flattening as Lacan says). And this is interesting. Because what can be demonstrated relatively easily is the relationship of the Borromean knot to other knots or loops as shown in the figure below. The three red intersection points are again on a circle (black), so with regard to the topologically equivalent triple cloverleaf loop on the right, the slurry has only been made visible in a different way.

The 'infinite' straight lines, which in the triple clover loop on the right side are not flattened, point to something else, namely to the real. The real forces itself upon us, because the combination of three 'infinite' straight lines now stands for the IRS, i.e. for imagining the symbolic real. And so one comes closer to *Analytic Psychocatharsis*, where the same thing is in the centre in a slightly different way, namely in the *formula-words* to be applied there. There it is also about a circle, on which different letters are lined up (see picture next to it). They also have a knot or certain interfaces which, just as in the Borromean knot, show, but also leave open the entire construction of the symbolic, imaginary and real.

While this openness to Lacan allowed him to explain his psychoanalytical theory of the unconscious theoretically, the *formula-words* present it in a form that is particularly suitable for practical application. I have already referred to the connections and comparisons of practice in psychoanalysis and *Analytic Psychocatharsis*. Thus, the same meditative element is found in evenly suspended attention and in the kind of 'free associations' in order to awaken the unconscious, as it happens in *Analytic Psychocatharsis* through the use of the *formula-words*. For the psychoanalyst   stagnations, promises, gestural interruptions, etc. are the interfaces that the unconscious causes in conversation and thus characterizes psychoanalytic discourse. In *Analytic Psychocatharsis*, the *formula-words* are written in a continuous stroke and circle, together with the structuring interfaces (shown again in the adjacent figure with the interfaces drawn in). And thus they also awaken the unconscious.

For when read from the respective interfaces, various meanings result from this formula word, which is written in Latin. It is the same kind of different meanings as they occur in the just mentioned stagnation in the flow of speech, psychological splittings or Freudian promises. Starting with the S in the upper right corner it is called SCIS / NOMEN, you know the name. Or beginning with M: MENS / CIS / NO, The Spirit, the Mind, this side of No. Or: OMEN SCIS N, you know the Omen N. And further: C IS NOMEN S, one hundred this name S etc. (I do not list them all here). As nonsensical as some of the meanings may be, they are grammatically and syntactically normal and even semantically okay, but they play no role in the further course of *Analytic Psychocatharsis*.

Important is only the uniform writing like E N S C I S N O M, which only has to be repeated meditatively, mentally, in thoughts, to stimulate the unconscious as mentioned. So I let the test persons meditate, but not according to any ideological, neuropsychological, 'spiritual' or purely conventional psychoanalytical guidelines. Everyone can read and study for themselves how the formula words have been developed from the concepts of linguistics, topology, psychoanalysis etc. and the meditative process as such (withdrawal from one's own everyday thoughts as in yoga, for example).

The individual meanings are only meaningful for this purpose; they are no longer needed for meditative practice. Here the respondent should only repeat, reverberate the uniform word formula, only the continuous writing mentally, i.e. purely in thoughts. Because the formula words (several are necessary for practising) do not prejudge anything, because the meanings are completely disparate, and yet scientifically constructed in the sense of the theory of early body mirroring and of the meaning of the imaginary and symbolic signifiers, they represent a new, well-founded, psychotherapeutic procedure. It has never been said so conclusively before.

It is particularly conclusive as a conclusion from psychoanalytic argumentation. Circle and 'infinite' straight line are the equivalent elements of Lacan's knot theories. But the relational elements, which manage in the relationship of the conscious to the unconscious, of the imaginary to the symbolic and thus also to the real, which thus form a quotient (S relates to I or vice versa), convey the essential. For the symbolic is supposed to be imagined in reality, i.e. the imaginative focus in meditation, the imaginary signifier of *Analytic Psychocatharsis* takes up speaking, the Id Speaks, from the unconscious in its overlapping linguistics being cut there. It accesses the phoneme composition, the letter-by-letter effect of the *formula-word* in the unconscious.[89]

---

[89] Oudée Dünkelsbühler, U., Zeugnis & Schrift: B(r)uchstaben an der Couch, Les Etats Généraux de la Psychanalyse (2001).

The letters broken through the intersections in the *for-mula-word* (and better called B(r)uchstaben) attack just such places in the unconscious. While an impulse in the form of an affect breaks through wordlessly into the consciousness, i.e. is only an expression of affect, the impulses are usually stored in the unconscious in what Freud called "ideational representative". They are picto-rial-word-actings, imaginary and symbolic signifiers, separated, cut, broken in various ways. Within these fragments a transition (Lacan: Transition) takes place, which makes it possible that the displaced and split-off parts can now become visible and conscious as a whole. These visible and audible wholenesses that have been pushed into consciousness are, of course, again the *pass-words*, since they have to do with the identity of the person concerned. They name his identity, his fit-ting.

This can again be seen in the Borromean knot, which is now a little more inscribed. If it is a matter of meaning, for example, it is due to the cut or the overlap between the symbolic and the imaginary. Since the formula words have no sense (they are built up of disparate meanings, but together they do not make any sense at all), they are particularly well suited to lure such a word out of the unconscious in the form of such a *pass-word*, or even to blackmail it. The meaning of the *pass-word* can be totally abstract, just as the words of ivory-tower scholars at the university or the directors of psychoana-

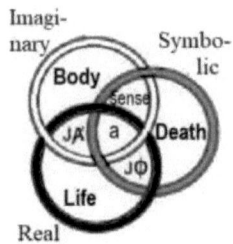

lytical institutes usually are.[90] But the *pass-words* also touch the object of desire (a) and the forms of enjoyment (YA and JΦ). YA is the 'Jouissance de L'Autre', the enjoyment of the Other, and JΦ is the 'jouissance phallique', better called 'plaisir phallique', because it has no access to true enjoyment. The *pass-words* have an equal part in everything.

---

[90] Freud said there's something paranoid about science. The sense present in the unconscious is - since it is supposedly too much subject-related - not affected. It is talked over.

## 9. Grand Delusion and Enjoyment

"La sagesse, c'est quoi?.. c'est le savoir de la 'jouis-sance',[91] which I can just barely translate: Wisdom is the knowledge about enjoying. And that is the very last, autochthonous enjoyment. Lacan distinguishes between three forms of enjoyment - according to his division of all being into the imaginary, the symbolic and the real - and says: the imaginary of enjoyment is bodily pleasure, the symbolic of enjoyment is the pleasure of speaking. And once again said: for the real of enjoyment Lacan's mathematicians are responsible, which I have replaced more practically by the exercises of *Analytic Psychocatharsis*, since for both the enjoyment lies in the IRS, in the real ( reality-related ) imagination of the symbol, the exactly fitting *pass-word*.

For plants and - as I have already quoted elsewhere - also for trees, amoebae and bacteria, a pleasure applies that is mainly fed by the imaginary, but a little bit of the real must be present. Of course, this is not the human form of the 'jouissance', which is close to the 'Ding' and hardly ever realized by anyone. Nevertheless, one can speak of 'jouisance' in the case of plants - and why not even in the material world of the universe - although it must be said that they completely lack the symbolic, and in this case especially the desire to speak. But the 'jouissance' throws sparks all the more in the image-creative, in the most illustrious Rays.

---

[91] Lacan. J., Seminaire XIX, seuil (2011) S. 169

So there is not yet much evidence of the desire to speak, so it can only be exercised by people who, as is well known, make use of it a lot: women at the market, men in the football club, but also everywhere else where gossip and chatting takes place, the desire to speak prevails. One can also emphasize the politicians and scientists, who believe to know everything and therefore believe to be wise in their enjoyment. Also here a little bit of the real thing must be present. Not only the mathematicians prove that. With the founders of religions and the quite advanced philosophers, but also with some natural scientists, the real is involved when they speak - with pleasure - of their discipline.

But all this is not the 'sagesse', the wisdom that knows about the real of enjoyment. Later, Lacan also said quite clearly that the ultimate 'jouissance' - in its most comprehensive and superordinate form, so to speak or in a form that summarizes them all.[92] He also spoke of the real enjoyment of the real Other, which is then the one without the crossed-out O. I have already indicated this in a simplified way with the concept of 'autochthonous enjoyment' that occurs everywhere and, above all, was already there, even if it only 'exists' as such - as Lacan says - i.e. it 'sists' (persists) from outside (ex). It can exist in the three mentioned forms, but my attempt goes there, to bridge the gap between the existence as pure being and the ex-existence as an own procedure of self-practice derived from Lacan's psychoanalysis, yes, to bring it directly to experience.

---

[92] Lacan, J., Seminar XXI, Vortrag vom 12. 3. 1974

This enjoyment, which is inherent in flora and which is also accessible to human experience, is however dominated by the imaginary, by physical pleasure. The enjoyment that occurs in the form of a self-sublimation of the aforementioned first exercise of *Analytic Psychocatharsis* is, however, much more complex in the human being than is possible in plants. The human brain and unconsciousness, which is so overflowing, is busy with edges and corners, colours and shimmering figures, signs and signals and much more, which you can experience immediately when you swallow a tiny little tablet of LSD. The hallucinatory mirror cabinet opens its doors. But it also makes you feel bodily pleasure, which is exceeded in self-sublimation, right up to the first flash of the 'jouissance'.

At this tipping point, where I also speak of the blissing, cathartic drizzling, the transition to the second exercise takes place. For catharsis cannot be held as a permanent state, something like this would be tantamount to a manic state, as it may have occurred in the past with mystics or in yoga, but under which a critical, rational consciousness suffers. Even in hypnosis, as Freud used it in the beginning for therapy, catharsis occurs, but it takes place in a hypnotic state. In this state the subject remains dependent on the voice of the therapist, the more he surrenders to the aforementioned body lust. The people only transformed their symptoms into a frenzy of dependence. The images remembered in hypnosis were then - woken up again - not valid for much, they seemed to be only half hallucinations to which one did not have to admit to.

Freud abandoned this method because he wanted the person who was mature from the outset, i.e. who was ready to speak and confess, to have the truth. But to get to these direct images through 'free associations' and interpretations proved to be difficult and time-consuming. However, catharsis occurring at the tipping point of the first exercise in *Analytic Psychocatharsis* is consciously experienced and helps to start the second exercise. In this exercise, the focus is on the Id Speaks, which is first perceived in the form of an Id Sounds which is an inner tone or sound. Lacan, for example, points out the 'sound' and the rhythmic proclamations that belong to the Real at several points in his seminars.[93] One can also understand the 'sound' as the primary process of the speech instinct, of the Speaks.

By concentrating on the inner 'sound' there is still a bit of catharsis, perhaps one can still speak of something hypomaniacal. However, after some time of this exercise of inner listening, word sounds, phrases and *passwords* will appear. This opens up a more direct path in which nothing can be repressed, denied and rejected so easily, since the primary processes of Rays and Speaks come together closely and leave no way out from the truth.

Displacement and rejection correlate closely with what is called a Grand Delusion (life lie). It becomes most obvious where one claims to tell the truth with special

---

[93] Lacan, J., Seminar II, Walter (1980) S. 327

effort. To say something quite clearly, polished with arguments, emphatically transparent and intent on conviction, is already close to a delusion or is itself a delusion. Even scientific talk usually arouses the suspicion that something is wrong with the truth. Even if it is not a blatant lie, the truth is at least lacking, because a feeling for language, a reference to the other, an authentic and yet differentiated speaking, which would include the other in the reasons, is missing. Even if speech is insufficient or diffuse, it isn't necessarily delusive, nor anything actually said. Seen in this way, the truth can actually only be half told.

The same applies to good understanding, which particularly affects the psychoanalyst when he easily attributes what his patient says between the lines to a hasty, short-circuited solution to the problem at hand. The market women mentioned above, who gossip among themselves, also understand each other perfectly, but of course this is not the understanding that is truthfully necessary. "I get along so well with my neighbour," said one, but in reality the market women only exchange superficialities, where there is not much to understand, but it unites. One can go completely crazy with all this understanding, and so it is perhaps not wrong to distinguish too good understanding from true understanding.

Even in a lecture, it is not always best when everything has been understood very well. Often it is better if you don't understand everything, but feel that there is something decisive about the lecture (and this was usually the case with Lacan). If one understands everything because it is already pre-chewed and simply said, one falls asleep prematurely. But if you notice what is special and important, what is new and correct that is being communicated, you keep your ears pricked up. You may not understand everything, but you have understood that there is something in what has been said that you can still clarify. If you have not fully grasped the content, you can read it later or listen to the whole thing again or ask again.

For the one who understands knows only what the other also thinks he knows. For example, today we know so much about National Socialism and the Third Reich, yet we have not yet understood what really happened.[94] Exactly this phenomenon is also a matter of the unconscious. For "the unconscious is the part of the concrete discourse as a supra-individual one, which is not available to the subject in restoring the continuity of his conscious discourse".[95] It is "the chapter of my history that has remained white or is occupied by a lie". It is the repressions that help us with this lie, which in the end can even become a grand delusion (Lebenslüge), which is helpful for death. Whoever has to constantly endure the battles of cover-up, embezzlement and pinocchio-like lies will not live that long.

---

[94] Maier, H., in der SZ vom 27.11.00, wo der Autor, ehemaliger Kultusminister in Bayern, diesbezüglich fragt: „Wie lernt man zu begreifen, was man schon weiß. (where the author, former Minister of Culture in Bavaria, asks in this regard: "How do you learn to understand what you already know. "

[95] Lacan, J., Schriften I, Walter (1980) S. 97- 98

However, even those who, like the double agents, are never allowed to lie, do not live too long. As mentioned at the beginning, they cannot erect a building of delusion, because they would get lost in it. Instead, from the very beginning, they reject the truth - the truth of their relationships with other humans - so completely, that they can only orient themselves according to one right and wrong. Of course, this is true for a great many people. For financial managers it is wrong to lose money, if necessary even fraud is the right thing to do. For politicians, everything they look at is always right, only the counterparties do everything wrong. The truth, which would span society, which would span all the relationships of people to other people, is discarded.

The worst thing - and this includes the examples above - is to lie to yourself, and yet almost everyone does it. Because mostly one does not recognize in time, where the core of the grand delusion is. It sits – expressed simply - in a complex of erotic-infantile basic striving on the one hand and aggressive striving on the other. However, both are so very differently structured, but together they form the original, unconsciously remaining fate-logo, which then comes out so splendidly in the passport words. Somewhere Freud once said that psychoanalysis is of little use in healing, but it is useful in finding the truth. In finding the truth lies the true enjoyment.

I believe I have shown that finding out what the saying "He is at the top of the o n e s" means involves both such enjoyment and truth-finding, and that I can therefore justifiably speak of the lust for truth. It is not a truth that has its validity primarily in social life, but rather one that should actually be called "o n e without a point". For it takes place first of all in the person concerned. Just how far he then goes out into society and publishes it, is his issue or another issue. In order to explain this further and better, I will report here on an additional example, which was also the *pass-word* of someone who had been practicing *Analytic Psychocatharsis* for a long time, and later I will quote an open, honest confession by Freud, which - especially as far as the truth is concerned - shows its true greatness.

"She already has her work clothes" sounded up from the depths of the just mentioned adept of *Analytic Psychocatharsis*, and he knew immediately what it was all about. By 'she' he meant the girlfriend he had known for a long time and intended to marry. And the term 'work clothes' was no problem either, he told me, because they consisted of nothing, just her naked skin, the entire surface of the sex appeal. As much as he was amazed at the appearance of such a *pass-word*, he was also shocked by the ironic, almost scornful truth of this saying, which degraded his girlfriend to a sex worker.

But he also felt an enlightening surprise at the uncouthness and directness of the expression. No friend, no therapist could have told him this so convincingly and unmaskingly. Especially no moralizer. Of course, the truth was also mocking, frivolous, a joke among men, but somehow it was also shameful. Above all, however, it belonged to him alone at first, and that made him happy, he really liked that. Finding his own truth detector within, was like a small sensation for him. He felt strongly motivated to tell me about it and to continue with the exercises.

But he also told his girlfriend soon after, whereupon both took a lot of time to talk about their relationship. Had he always seen her that way? Was it possible to talk openly about fantasies that everyone had about their relationship? How often do you just not find the right word, the right beginning of a conversation? One has to evoke the truth detector within oneself, but this does not work in the usual way of a premeditation or an effort of will with best intentions. If you can tell a dream when the other person knows how to interpret it, this may be a similarly good introduction to deeper and honest communication. But who can do this? Even the psychoanalyst must often hear entire series of dreams in order to be able to give an accurate interpretation.

On the other hand, the *pass-words*, which are set in motion by the revealing structure of the *formula-words*, are an ideal stimulus for self-awareness, self-analysis and extended communication. They have to do with the linguistics of lies, but also with that of truth. That she "has always had her work clothes", with this my respondent exposed the delusion that women like to work in these clothes of nothing. Everything is already there, the girlfriend only needs to get going, ironically said. My respondent knew very well that this was not true, but he had not understood it, as I mentioned above about the history of the Third Reich. Also in the unconscious we know everything, also in sleep we often know that we are dreaming, and even if we have understood this knowledge, we have not grasped it.

I have already mentioned this phenomenon using the example of the lucid dream, in which, as I said, one knows that one is dreaming, but this thought easily swirls back into normal dreaming or back to sleep. The physicist F. A. Wolf has described this well in his book 'The Physics of Dreams' - contradicting himself.[96] He tells how he encounters children in a lucid dream and explains to them how he can grasp through all things (a typical ability in this state), but at that moment he has already forgotten that the children are not really children at all, but only dreamt ones, and so he is wrong twice: imaginary children and imaginary grasping through, so he is nearly in sleep again. So what does he actually want to say?

He wants to say that he knows something, that he has understood something, but he has not grasped, comprehended it. He hasn't grasped what it's really all about, and so he's just rambling on about identity problems, that seem to be solved in the lucid dream. One is reminded of brainwashing with the help of which the Chinese today want to reorient the Uyghurs into dolls loyal to the Chinese party. They have understood nothing about human identity, in which the truth will prevail and the Uighurs will remain Uighurs. In the passport words, you don't always understand your identity very well, but they help us to grasp it more and more.

---

[96] Wolf, F.A., The Physics of Dreams, Byblos Verlag (1995)

And furthermore: when I quoted Freud above with the sentence "feeling of happiness when satisfying a wild, Ego-unrestrained urge", I must add that Freud also emphasizes body-related, existential enjoyment there. Precisely this is not the case with substitute satisfaction and tamed, 'goal-inhibited' drive satisfaction, and the untamed can never and nowhere be implemented directly, because the human constitution, social rules and cultural achievements are opposed to this. In *Analytic Psychocatharsis*, however, there is a body-related enjoyment, namely catharsis, which satisfies the urge quite 'the other way round', even if this is not completely sufficient. Increased by self-sublimation, the drive stimulus finds a direct path into what Freud calls "perceptual identity", i.e. the most primordial area of the psychic, but this time not only in the form of the hallucination of an underlying desire (a desire-related 'ray'), but also of pure enjoyment that can also speak (a 'ray/'speaks').

This 'radiance/speech' is liberated from the proximity of psychosis, because it is subject - as Freud says - to the "guardian of our mental health", the " censor", which is effective even in sleep and emanates from something that is located between E flat resistance, the I and superego. The "censor" prevents us from waking up in the morning as something completely different from what we went to bed with in the evening afore. And so, even in the half-awake state of meditation, it helps to prevent thoughts other than those of the *formula-words* from constantly taking over. Only in those short moments when the "censor" gives way a little bit, thoughts of the world and also the *pass-words* come to light, which can be checked rationally for a short time, or which can be received and kept as interesting.

I must admit, however, that a good psychoanalysis can produce equally good solutions. For example, I mention Freud's own dream regarding his son in World War I.[97] After some association and open interpretation, Freud admits here that despite the "painful emotion when such a misfortune [the son might have been wounded or fallen] really happened," a reawakening of envy of youth, almost a hidden death wish, might ease the pain. This is an incredibly honest and open description, as it is simply necessary in any therapy. As much as the conventional psychoanalytic procedure is circumstantial and longwinded, I advise anyone who is deeply involved in *Analytic Psychocatharsis* to spend at least fifty hours of analytical psychotherapy and to consult extensive literature on the subject.

I have invented the Formula- and *pass-words* because they come even closer to the truth, as the example with the work clothes shows. Further clear and precise arguments are not necessary. The Formula- and *pass-words* do not lie. They do not tell the truth themselves, but they make it possible, just like the algorithms do. But compared to the algorithms that Harari foresees for the future by renewing and changing themselves mutually and completely undermining the individual of today, the Formula- and *pass-words* are transparent in their inter-

---

[97] Freud, S., GW II/III, S. 564 (Freud dreamt of news of his son's death, but it did not really happen).

face structure. They cannot unfold a life of their own, but only the life of those who call themselves their own.

So in summary, once more I show the scheme of lines of force (circle line and infinite straight line). One can see the vertical as the real, the horizon as the symbolic and the diagonal circle as the imaginary. The *formula-words* have something to do with the diagonal circle. They are purely formal-symbolic, and in their simple interface drawing they are insinuated pictorial-imaginary. But they push out the real, the vertical, from which the horizontal and the diagonal now-more also get a new value. This is expressed cathartically in the new vertical ('trickling down through') and worthily in the new horizontal. The whole thing closes in the diagonal and repeats itself further in the trinity of the Borromean knot or O. Count Wittgenstein's three-part unification.

My teaching analyst O. Count Wittgenstein described this in his book "saying, hearing, seeing".[98] In it, he used myths and fairy tales as well as philosophical and psychoanalytical forms of observation to formulate what he called a 'trialogical' (three-conversational) goal. The picture below from his book shows this in an overview. 'Trialogical' should mean that the in itself (as in Lacan's

[98] Wittgenstein, O. Graf, sagen, hören, sehen, (saying, hearing, seeing) Band I, Bonz (1978)

threefold knot) 'three-partited' human being can find a unity through a special kind of mediation or through the 'logical practice' of psychoanalysis in the form of a three-conversational logo and not just of a dialogue. For it is not enough that only the therapist and the patient sit together (this would again result in the two autistic persons), there must also be a third person or a Third Party in the room in the sense of the three-conversational : S. Freud, for example, or the consensus of psychoanalytic teaching. Only in this way, by means of a psychoanalytical 'working through' of the tripartite nature of the X-, Y- and Z-axes, can man reach self-unity in a comprehensive form, to a personality that is uniformly at rest within itself.

The same applies to *Analytic Psychocatharsis*, for which I have described Wittgenstein's and Lacan's versions in my book 'teadrunken'. In this context I can once again make a final statement on the 'Ding', because it also has something to do with the trialogical. I see the 'Ding' as the counterpart, an opposite supplement to the predominance of the symbolic-real in psychoanalysis, especially in the Lacanian form. Thus, in 'Ding' there is an emphasis on the imaginary-real, but a third results from it, whereby, apart from the trialogue, the fundamentally triadic (Wittgenstein's Trinitarian) is aimed at.[99]

---

[99] When one speaks of the triad in psychoanalysis, one always means the Oedipal configuration of father, mother and child.

And with this I refer again to the individual who practices *Analytic Psychocatharsis*. He, his 'Ding', is ultimately the third. Even those who believe that they cannot learn and master the method all by themselves can of course consult a therapist who knows the method or who favours an analytical approach. Sooner or later, however, one will pursue it alone or participate in the further development of *Analytic Psychocatharsis*. Because it is just as important to teach others as it is to teach yourself. After all, it is similar to classical psychoanalysis. Freud himself, in his plea for "lay analysis", advocated that anyone who has had experience with his method could also become a therapist. Now, however, few patients become analysts themselves later on, although they have gained a lot of experience and the method I developed especially in connection with astro- and eco-psychoanalysis makes it easier for the layman to become a co-scientist.

## 10. Involuntary Soliloquies

Simple entertainment is the death of the vertical. In entertainment, only something is scattered in the horizontal, which remains without consequences. The vertical wants to say something, confirm something, acknowledge something, appreciate something. It has to do with the 'Ding' that the triad understands as an objective kind of dignity. Writers who still know something about poetry, that is, about poetry, epic poetry, symbolic wealth or other forms of great narrative art, will always appreciate the vertical. Such as Peter Handke, who shortly before receiving the Nobel Prize for Literature in November 2019 was visited by P. Kümmel, an editor of the weekly German newspaper DIE ZEIT.[100]

The two talked about the fact that Handke often used the expression 'u. S.' in his diaries. That was an abbreviation for 'involuntary self-talk', Handke said. He wrote down thoughts that came to him spontaneously, so to speak without warning. It is not a conscious, linear process of thought, of conscious reflection. When I read this, my association was immediately that these, in our opinion, perfectly matched the explanation of the *pass-words* in *Analytic Psychocatharsis*. In the first exercise, while paying attention to an inner, lucid experience, a brightness, a point of the Rays, one repeats the formula words until this cathartic perception leads to clear relaxation,

---

[100] Kümmel, P., Was bedeutet (what means) ‚u.' ‚S.' ?, DIE ZEIT vom 2. 12. 2019, S. 44

e.g. of the said 'trickling through'. But then follows the 'involuntary soliloquy'.

In the second exercise of this procedure, as already mentioned, this catharsis is used, in which one listens inwardly to the 'tone', 'sound', to the 'Id Sounds', 'id Speaks'. In the end, the same thing happens as with Handke's 'involuntary self-talk'. Most people talk to themselves arbitrarily and intentionally, at least for a short time, during or after exciting, emotional and moving incidents. In doing so, one consciously plays through something by talking to oneself and assuming an imaginary listener. But an 'involuntary self-talk' is something completely different.

One is in a slightly pensive state, in which a few memories may emerge, pale reminiscences, not any concrete thoughts. Perhaps a half word comes into consciousness, which suddenly turns into a half-loudly perceived thought, which sounds strange, coming to you as if from far away and then being clearly received and confronted with a now conscious thought. After all, one must somehow respond to such a thought, perceived in a low voice, especially if it was articulated involuntarily, i.e. as if it were foreign or from somewhere else. Because then one has already grasped this thought as belonging to oneself. It concerns one, it affects one. It is not a sober, lifeless, improper thought.

It is one that, despite its oddity, is immediately taken up, replied to or accepted as appropriate. Handke must have known hundreds of such moments, although he never exercised *Analytic Psychocatharsis*, in which such soliloquies also occur, which can now also be called 'involuntary', but which were deliberately initiated, provoked and urged to surrender. The involuntariness lies in the 'hearing of thoughts' of the *pass-word* that finally comes about, which is a creative achievement of the unconscious and thus nothing self-made, self-thought and deliberately produced.

As a poet, however, one is probably constantly in a universe of vocabulary, words, phrases, half and whole sentences, semantems and light deliriums that trigger the poet's creativity. Lacan speaks of "ultra-reduced phrases" in this respect, because the unconscious hardly ever allows longer word passages. If the ancient prophets experienced whole paragraphs as sent by God and rendered them verbally, they just mixed a combination of short phrases with their own thoughts expressed from ancient times and by significant ancestors. They did not notice the process of mixing. When they were dominated by a problem for days, when they had heard God speak in their dreams, they pronounced this perfectly analogous to it.

The prophet Eliphas, for example, was one of the three friends of Job. But as is well known, the three were only ultra-orthodox know-it-alls who wanted to teach Job in an arrogant professorial tone when he was in a bad way, even though he believed in God with particular piety. The God of Job was still a personified power, a soul-spiritual forefather, the voice of the Jewish political clan, which held people together in a bad and right way. The psychoanalyst C.G. Jung saw in Job's God a split personality, in which the split of the human self is reflected and which could no longer be solved by piety, but only by therapy. In this way the events of Job could perhaps be formulated psychoanalytically. But such observations do not solve the problems of modern man. The prophecies of the past are not those of today.

Job is involved in the imaginary- and the symbolic-real. His outward success as a land- and herd-owner makes him wallow in the 'excess' of his wealth and potency, and so he loses himself in the 'real illusion' of early childhood attitudes. For Job's God "exists" although he is not there, i.e. he 'sits', exists, insists, 'ex', outside: even outside language and images. This idea of God refers less to the 'symbolic father', who is present as just an absent person. He is much more fully real, indeed the real par excellence, outside of all the usual and other psychoanalytical attributions. "In a subtle way this real God also undermines the symbolic 'castration'; the necessary separation from the primordial Other," the separation from the early mother, "it is fended off, if not even denied," writes theologian Schneider-Harpprecht, who wants to justify her faith with it.[101]

But I also see in this a chance for the explanation of 'involuntary soliloquies' and for the *Analytic Psychocatharsis*, which in their *formula-words* are with one foot still insistent and with the other 'ex', situated from the

---

[101] Schneider - Harpprecht, U., Mit Symptomen leben, eine andere Perspektive der Psychoanalyse J. Lacans (Living with symptoms, a different perspective on psychoanalysis by J. Lacan) (2000)

language. Thus the aforementioned Eliphas once said - probably to confirm his views - that the following happened to him at night, in the darkness of half-asleep: "A word was brought to me surreptitiously, and my ear then acquired a whisper of it". This made him shudder and tremble, and he said that "the hair of his flesh began to bristle,"[102] a clear case of 'trickling' catharsis. It may sound astonishing, but in these two Old Testament statements the nature of 'involuntary soliloquy' and *Analytic Psychocatharsis* is described from a completely different angle. The first statement refers to the Speaks (whispering), the second to the Rays (the shuddering, 'trickling through').

But Eliphas does not take the chance to create a self-analytical procedure out of it or to write a book like Handke. He saves himself from the emerging fear, from this primal effect, from which the infant escapes into the 'real illusion' or into the symbolism of the relationship with his mother, into his God. In this way, Eliphas finds the "most moving form of interrupted discourse, namely the law as misunderstood," as advanced,[103] as denying the primal repression. I have mentioned $\Phi$ above as the sexual metaphor, but it is also described by Lacan as the interrupter of the discourse of the sexes. Here, with Job and Eliphas, the placard God is the interrupter, the Lord-Signifier, to which Eliphas adheres, and which is derived from exemplary ancestors and mythical laws. In the hearing of voices and 'trickling through' Eliphas was

---

[102] Job 4, 12 und 15
[103] Lacan, J., Seminar II, Walter (1980) S. 166

still present as something 'ex-sisting', original-originating, but already in the next moment he begins to hold a monologue, which he passes off as a prophecy of his God. He falls back into speculative insistence.

The law as misunderstood is mythical-magical, it is not questioned and worked through by reflection or meditation. Eliphas' statements clearly show that he only stubbornly adheres to the religious rules, which he does not see through. He only chants them, while Job believes he can see through them and rejects them in this hollowed-out form. He wants to lead them back to their original essence. Job really meets the 'ex-sisting', this very real other, who is impersonal, not a private God, but a negation. "There is a lack in the Other, (written as a crossed out O, ($\emptyset$), and that which is missing is a signifier. God is missing an explanation for the evil in the world."[104] There's the rub. It is 'ex', and what is 'suspended' is the general discourse that should be carried on beyond the sexual discourse in order not to be interrupted.

The general discourse, "language per se," says philosopher M. Heidegger on this subject, "speaks of man. . . It speaks as the ringing of silence". . . . We 'speak' in waking and in dreams. We 'speak' always, even when we do not utter a word, but only listen or read, even when we ... are at work or at leisure. We 'speak' constantly in some way. We 'speak' because 'speaking' is natural to us', because only 'as a speaker' is the human being: hu-

---

[104] Lacan-entziffern.de

man".[105] So it is no wonder and something completely natural what Handke does when he 'involuntary talks to himself' and plays semi-meditative games of thought in words.

Philosopher P. Sloterdijk called this process a 'unity of guarding and thinking' and traced it back to the Greek word sophronein (to consider). Thus, philosopher M. Heidegger also tried to "put philosophising back into the pre-socratic state, in which ... this unity of guarding and thinking was still possible".[106] Sloterdijk also calls it a "pro-confused unity", because the later occidental thinking without guards as well as the East Asian guarding without thinking only caused confusion. In addition to Heidegger, Sloterdijk also mentions Foucault and F. v. Weizsäcker, who 'came closest to the paradoxical ideal of a presocratism at the level of contemporary knowledge'.

With this I can return to *Analytic Psychocatharsis*. In it the self-talks are initiated by the reverberation of the formula words and let the so-called *pass-words* emerge from the unconscious. Once again a very last example, which perhaps fits quite well here. Some time ago I heard the following phrase or short sentence during analytical-psychocathartic meditation: "Give it to me in writing". Give it to me in writing, it, the speaks? Can I have it in writing, you, my readers? Yes, of course, I

---

[105] Heidegger, M., Unterwegs zur Sprache (on the way to language), Verlag G. Neske (1993) S. 32-33

[106] Sloterdijk, P., Du musst dein Leben ändern (you need to change your life) , Suhrkamp (2009) S. 272 - 275

want it in writing, that which is about me, about my books and the method of *Analytic Psychocatharsis* I have developed. In writing, because that will cause true 'jouissance'.

After such a *pass-word*, one automatically conducts a short self-talk, which is not a banal, conscious everyday palaver, but a therapy session, an important thought from offstage, a creativity that is no longer entirely worldly. Of course, not every *pass-word* is a divine revelation, some don't mean anything to you, or you can't work on them rationally enough. This is often necessary, although it is not as difficult and irrelevant as with most dream sayings or the prophecies of Pythia in the Delphic Oracle. When interpreting dreams, the psychoanalyst usually has to work on whole dream sequences that drag on for months, and with Pythia it was the priests who - probably mostly in their own sense - gave the final interpretation of the prophecies.

I am convinced that Handke found inspiration for his writing activity through his 'involuntary soliloquies' in the same way as in the case of the *pass-words*. He also did not need any more *Analytic Psychocatharsis*, he had developed a self-analytical procedure in himself, or rather it has developed in that way in him. But most people are not writers with a Nobel Prize background, and I can confidently recommend my method to them. They would get better results, because Handke has never described or explained exactly how he conducts his 'involuntary self-talks', whereas the method of *Analytic Psy-*

*chocatharsis* can be learned from the few pages in the appendix alone.

## Appendix

The procedure of *Analytic Psychocatharsis* is very simple from its practical side - as already described in part. Nevertheless, I will give here a short summary and further formula words.[107] You sit in a comfortable posture and repeat one, two or up to five formula words slowly one after the other purely in your mind, while at the same time you pay attention to whether something appears that has the character of an 'Id *Rays*'. The "ray" can be an enlightenment, body image perception, a shimmer, a 'spot of light', or a basic lucidity that is associated with such a phenomenon. So the ray is not something one has to imagine, create or even force oneself. It is present in every human being as the primary form of a drive (scopic-drive) and thus only has to be awakened or expected. In the same way, a 'trickling through' can also be felt or the sensation can emerge how one's own body image shifts,[108] widens or is simply fixed as black paint, as a stain in front of the closed eyes. Because

---

[107] Further formula words can be found in other publications or on the website given below. For the time being, these are sufficient. You should not need more than five.

[108] This is an experience that has something to do with atavistic emotional reactions. The early humans still felt a lot with their uncovered skin, touched it and communicated in an environment-related way. Even with moving pieces of music, when it grips you like a shiver trickling down your back, we fall back on these particularly deep emotions. In *Analytic Psychocatharsis*, however, this experience is used as confirmation of an insight, e.g. in the *pass-words*.

black is already a perception, which can stand out from the darkness in the head quite slightly. No matter what is 'seen' or 'experienced', it will have the character of even a very small 'Id *Rays*', and that is enough.

Thus a relaxation occurs, a catharsis, a liberation experience, which can be increased especially if at the same time the said *formula-words* are practiced purely mentally. At the bottom left one can see a different Formula-Word as I have given in the main text. Also this (RA-DIC-IT) is not a normal word from Latin, but it contains several overlapping meanings in one formulation, it is 'linguistically crystalline' like Lacan said from the unconscious. Besides the radiat and dicit (rays and speaks) there are several disparate meanings written in a circle and read from different letters. For example, here one can also use "adi cit r" (approach, it moves R), "C i tradi" ( handed over a hundred i), "citra di" (on this side the gods), "dicit ra" (it says ra), "r adic it" (add r, it goes), "radi cit" (get scratched, it moves), "trad ici" (tell, I have met) etc., whereby much sounds quite absurd. But this has no meaning for the formal expression. It is only decisive to be able to clearly explain the scientific reasoning (several meanings in one formulation, usage only of other interfaces), and this is very important for the procedure, because this is the only way to have full confidence in the method.

This is the first exercise which is based on actual guidelines of psychoanalysis, because mental reverberation generates a regression (an inner retreat) which at the same time concentrates only on a narrowed aspect of the perceptual instinct (the *Rays*). In addition, *formula-word* repetition takes the place of what in psychoanalysis is called the obligation to repeat, the unconscious repetition. This is at least abolished as long as the exercises of the *Analytic Psychocatharsis* are effective. I have already indicated in the main text that this simplifies and reduces an essential hurdle of classical psychoanalysis. It is important that it comes to a catharsis, to a liberation experience and not only to a simple relaxation. At least for some time one frees oneself from the unconscious obligation to repeat.

As far as other forms of therapy and their problems are concerned, by using *Analytic Psychocatharsis* it is usually possible to avoid them in a simplified way. It is no longer enough simply to believe a therapist or meditation teacher and follow his simple instructions. Nowadays it is also necessary to understand that the method has a scientific basis and that one can and should participate with own thoughts. This way, in deeper moments of the exercises dependencies on the ideology of the method, on the teacher or therapist or irrational fears do not occur. The Id *Rays* (crystalline) of the cathartic experience are thus derived from the basic power of the scopic drive. It is therefore something that is originally present in every human being, just like the Id *Speaks* (the linguistic, the uttering).[109]

---

[109] In psychoanalysis we assume that symbolic order or language plays a decisive role in human development, dividing

After the R-A-D-I-C-I-T, the formula word O-R-S-A-C-E-R-A-M can be added, because if someone is really interested in learning the analytic pychocathartic method, at least three of these formulations are necessary. Two or even just one would tire one out too quickly. In the *formula-word* C-E-R-A-M-O-R-S-A (picture previous page) - once written differently - there are following meanings depending on the initial letter: C eram orsa (I was a hundred times beginning, amo R sacer (I love the holy R), cera morsa (the fragmented wax), mors acer (death is bitter), amor sacer (love is holy), etc.). As emphasized, one can forget these meanings immediately again. They are too disparate, i.e. cannot be reduced to any denominator. For if one practices them in the uniform lettering, one will never bring together the bitter death with the fragmented wax and the hundredfold beginning in one meaning. It is only important to understand how the *formula-words* are structured, so that one can scientifically-intellectually question the process at any time. If any feelings or ideas arise that are inappropriate or frightening, one can reflect or read more about the process. Blind faith is not required.

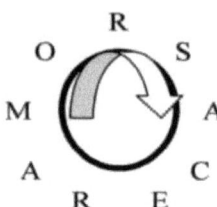

---

perception into a pure sensory activity and a drive activity. The activity of the senses is a real perception, the activity of instinct a pleasure of perception, in summary we speak of perceptiveness. The true comes in through language (It *Speaks*), the perception through reality (It radiates).

In the second exercise, attention is now paid to exactly this *Speaks*, this body echo, i.e. to a sound coming from above / right in the head, to a tone, sound, from the deep inside. After all, these are letters that emanate from this 'typographic' space and which the unconscious holds stored there. And it is precisely into this space that the *formula-words* have penetrated and have awakened and evoked the letters in their 'B(r)uchstaben'-likeness (broken-letterings). Again, the same applies here: it is a completely original aspect of the drive to express or speak, which is present in every human being as a primary process and even takes on the form of very brief, compact "inner sentences", "ultra-reduced phrases" in the unconscious (all concepts of Lacan for this phonetic experience).

Here, too, at first only a fine noise, a distant sound or similar can be perceived, but the practitioner will notice from the beginning that this is a concentration on a more up-right or up-central hearing system in the head. The echoes of the body have a relationship to this, which is being referred to here. Even if the actual hearing and speech system in the head is left-handed, the more rudimentary, musical and more regression accessible hearing and speech system is present on the right side and its echo structure is clearly recognizable. The short phrases of the *pass-words* are more suitable for this, while the left-sided system (psychoanalytically: the preconscious) plays a role in the longer ones.

If you read something about psychoanalysis and keep in touch with literary, scientific and other cultures, and have also read the present text, made an attempt with the exercises, in short: if you are a bit of an educated citizen, you will interpret the often immediately visible *pass-words* correctly. Thus Freud writes that even some dreams, which are now much more distorted than the *pass-words*, and which come directly from the symbolic-real, could be read directly from the "sheet". It is no longer necessary to ask the dreamer about his ideas and to bring in cumbersome interpretations.

And one last hint, which is often asked for. If one notices during the application of *Analytic Psychocatharsis* that the it *Rays* portion during practice is too strong, one switches to the it *Speaks* exercise and vice versa. Otherwise, both exercises should only be performed for about twenty minutes. The change between practical experience and theoretical thinking is important because in the end something in common will emerge: a mental self-awareness, a practical logic, a cathartic analysis. In the end, both exercises find their way to an inner 'mission', to a certainty of 'What about the ONE',[110] and thus to the possibility of being able to participate in the procedure.

On the other hand, I have already described that sometimes one does not only deviate from the meditative process in thoughts. Sometimes one even deviates between the individual formula words to images, memories, to a mixture of both and to *pass-words*, and yet re-

---

[110] This concerns the title of my book, also published in English, which deals with the same subject by means of literature and mathematics.

turns to formula word reversion. The advanced student will experience this as enriching, because he does not allow himself to be seduced into a one-sided direction of radiation or speech, but remains in the progression in the narrow combination of the two basic drives, basic principles, mirroring- and echo-discourse.

I have described several examples of these *pass-words* in the text. Everybody has to be patient and try out what he thinks is a safe word can. Sometimes it's like you're almost in retrospect, in the final phase of the *pass-word* experience, the phrase-hearing the short sentence. Sometimes it seems it's a very, very quiet thought, but still is clear or quite clear. I have to be so vague here, nevertheless there is no doubt about the phenomenon both from the psychoanalytic theory as well as from the many experiences I have collected. Even though the actual hearing-talking system in the head is laid out on the left-side, the right side is more rudimentary, musical and is prone to better regression, and its echo-structure has increased visibility.

Again: After the first exercise, the mental repetition of several formula words with a simultaneous occurrence thereof, see if you have a ray, a lucidity, a trickle, a liberating, cathartic experience, then you move on to the second exercise. Here you concentrate on the sound, the tone, the *Speaks* from above or right inside until you have completely transcended body-consciousness. If you notice that the ray portion of the training is too strong, you switch to the Speech Exercise and vice versa. Each exercise should be performed for about twenty minutes.

The aim of the procedure is to achieve an ideal, success-ful and satisfying combination of the two exercises. I cannot make any definite specifications here, because when the *Ray* and *Speaks* exercises are fulfilled in their combination, you should be able to notice it yourself. After all, the experiences mature in progress with the theory, the latter would require reading and engage-ment. The exchange of practical experience and theoret-ical thinking is important, because in the end something in common will emerge: a mental self-awareness, a practical logic, a cathartic analysis. Ultimately, both ex-ercises can also lead to an inner 'assignment', to a cer-tainty of being able to participate in the shaping of the procedure.

# Bibliography

Baggini, J., Ich denke, also will ich, (I think, so I want) dtv (2016)

Barkhaus, A., Mayer, M., Identität, Leiblichkeit, Normativität (identity, corporeality, normativity( Suhrkamp (1996)

Bauriedl, T., Beziehungsanalyse, (relationship analysis) Suhrkamp (1993)

Benthien, C., Wulf, Ch., Körperteile (body parts), Rowohlt (2001)

Bezzel, C., Wittgenstein, Junius (1996)

Breuer, R., Immer Ärger mit dem Urknall (Always Trouble with the Big Bang), Rowohlt (1993)

Brockman, J., Vogel, S., Wie funktioniert die Welt? (How does the world work), Fi-scher Taschenbuch (2013)

Byung-Chul Han, Die Austreibung des Anderen (The Expulsion of the Other), Fischer Wissenschaft (201)

Byung-Chul Han, Die Errettung des Schönen (The Salvation of Beauty), Fischer Wissenschaft (201)

Camus, A., Der Mythos des Sisyphos, Rowohlt (2018)

Carnap, R., Einführung in die Philosophie der Naturwissenschaft (Introduction to the Philosophy of Natural Science) (1969)

Damasio, A. R., Descartes` Irrtum, Dtv (1997)

Dennet, D. C., Von den Bakterien zu Bach – und zurück, Suhrkamp (2018)

Davies, P., Gott und die moderne Physik (God and modern physics), Bert. M. (1986)

Eccles, J. C., Gehirn und Seele, Piper (1987)

Eichmeier, J., Höfer, O., Endogene Bildmuster, U&S – Verlag (1974)

Fischer-Lichte, E., Performativität: Eine Einführung, transcript (2012)

Freud, S., Studienausgabe, Fischer (1989)

Goel, B. S. Meditation und Psychoanalyse, Ariston (1989)

Görz, G., Einführung in die Künstliche Intelligenz (Introduction to Artificial Intelligence), Addison-Wesley (1996)

Harari, Y. N., Homo Deus, C. H. Beck (2017)

Heidegger, M., Unterwegs zur Sprache, G. Neske (1959)

Hilbrecht, H., Meditation und Gehirn, Schattauer (2010)

Hofstadter, D., Die Analogie, Klett-Cotta (2014)

Horgan, J., An den Grenzen des Wissens, Luchterhand (1997)

Hustvedt, S., Die gleissende Welt (The blazing Wiorld) Rowohlt (2016)

Husttvedt, S., Das Leiden eines Amerikanmers, Rowohlt (2009)

Hustvedt, S., Wenn Gefühle auf Worte treffen (When feelings meet words ) , Kampa (2019)

Jacobs, A., Schrott, R., Gehirn und Gedicht, Hanser (2011

Jakobson, R., Semiotik, Suhrkamp (1988)

Jakobson, R., On Language, Harvard University Press (1995)

Jung. C.G., Gesammelte Werke, Walter (1983)

Kant, I., Kritik der reinen Vernunft, Reclam (1966)

Kluge, F., Etymologisches Wörterbuch, W. de Gruyter (1989)

Lacan, J., Schriften I - III, Walter, (1975)

Lacan, J., Seminare I,I, VII, XI, XX, Quadriga (1980-1995)

Lacan, J., Seminaire Nr. III, Iv, VIII, XVII, Edition Seuil (1981-1994)

Lacan, J., Die Bildungen des Unbewussten, Turia & Kant (2006)

Lacan, J., Mitschriften der Seminare,VI,IX,X,XII,XV, B.R.L.F., Strasbourg

Laplanche, J., Pontalis, J. B., Das Vokabular Der Psychoanalyse, Suhrkamp (1989)

Linke, D., Kunst und Gehirn, Rowohlt (2001)

Maar, C., Pöppel, E., Christaller, T., Die Technik auf dem Weg zur Seele, Rowohlt (1996)

Merleau-Ponty, M., Das Sichtbare und das Unsichtbare (The Visible and the Invisible) Fink Verlag (1994)

Pinker, S., Der Sprachinstinkt, Kindler (1996)

Plato, Sämtliche Werke, Insel Verlag (1991)

Popper, K. R., Eccles, J. C., Das Ich und sein Gehirn, Piper (1989)

Potthoff, P., Die Begegnung der Subjekte (The Encounter of Subjects), Psychosozial-Verlag (2014)

Roazen, D., Der innere Sinn, Archäologie eines Gefühls (The Inner Touch, Archaeology of Feeling), Fischer (2012)

Roheim, G., Die Panik der Götter (The Panic of the Gods), Kindler (1975)

Rosset, C., Das Reale in seiner Einzigartigkeit (The real in its uniqueness), Merve (2000)

Rüdinger, D., Perrez, M., Anthropologische Aspekte der Psychologie, O. Müller (1979)

Rudgley, R., Abenteuer Steinzeit, Kremaye & Scheriau (2001)

Schmidt-Hellerau, C., Lebenstrieb & Todestrieb (Life Drive & Death Drive), Libido & Lethe, Verlag Intern. Psychoanalyse (1995)

Searle, J. R., Geist, Hirn und Wissenschaft, Suhrkamp (1992)

Seidler, G. H., Der Blick des Anderen (The View of the Other), Verlag Intern, Psychoanalyse (1995)

Sinz, R., Gehirn und Gedächtnis, Fischer Utb (1981)

Strowik, E., Sprechende Körper (Speaking Bodies), Fink-Verlag (2009)

Thompson, R. F., Das Gehirn, Spectrum (1994)

Thorne, K. S., Gekrümmter Raum und Verbogene Zeit, Knaur (1996)

Tipler, F. J., Über die Omegapunkttheorie, Piper (1994)

Uexküll, Th., Fuchs, M., Subjektive Anatomie, Schattauer (1994)

Weiss, Der Andere in der Übertragung (The Other in Transference), Frommann-Holzboog, (1988)

Weizsäcker, C. F. von, Die Einheit der Natur (The Unity of Nature), Dtv (1995)

Weinberg, S., Der Traum von der Einheit des Universums, Bertelsmann (1993)

Weizenbaum, J., Die Macht der Computer, Stw (1977)

Wiener, O., Probleme der Künstlichen Intelligenz, Merve (1990)

Wilhelm, R., Informatik, C.H.Beck (1996)

Wilson, E. O., Der Wert der Vielfalt, Piper (199

Wolf, F. A., Die Physik der Träume, Byblos (1996)

Wygotski, L.S., Denken und 'Sprechen (Thinking and 'Speaking)', Fischer (1981)

# Books published in English by the author

**The physically sick Soul**
In this booklet of only forty pages, the author describes in a simplified form the method of Analytic Psychocatharsis that he developed. It is not only about the mentally ill soul, but also about the treatment of the disorder expressed in a more physical form.

**What about the ONE**
The One is only insufficiently described in mathematics. It is about the spiritual-physical unity of man, which can only be achieved through a combination of psychoanalytical and meditative exercises. The author describes this process using the literature of Siri Hustvedt and other female authors as well as the psychoanalysis of J. Lacan.

# Further books by the author from MCS-Verlag

## *Analytic Psychocatharsis*

Psychoanalytic theory and cathartic meditation cannot simply be transferred into each other. If, however, both methods are related by a decisive element (formula words containing several meanings in one stroke), a new method of one's own can be established. Psychoanalysis and meditative methods are discussed, and the practice of one's own procedure is described in detail.

## The Revolt of the Self

The classical method of analysis of the unconscious represents a too theoretical revolt of the self. In order to be successful in practice, a more direct self-analytic procedure is required, which everyone can develop out of themselves. Formulations that contain several meanings in a single stroke of writing can break up the unconscious of each individual through mental practice and free him or herself.

**'teadrunken'** The starting point of the book is the doctrine of the psychoanalyst O. Earl Wittgenstein, who assumed that man contains three parts within himself, which he can only combine in different ways to form a unity or uniform personality. He calls the ultimate and ideal unity the 'trialogue'. On the basis of the description of several mountain climbs, the author roams through all possible cultural and psychological questions in order to achieve the 'trialogue' through hiking, meditation and intellectual processing.

### Yoga and Psychoanalysis

Based on a scientific biography of the religious scientist and yoga teacher Kirpal Singh (Surat Shand Yoga), all forms of yoga are compared from the perspective of psychoanalysis. It is necessary to establish a procedure of one's own, which the author also calls *Analytic Psychocatharsis*. Numer-ous pictures and diagrams make the book attractive.